ANCIENT EGYPTIAN GARDENS

ANCIENT EGYPTIAN GARDENS

John Bellinger

Amarna Publishing

First published in 2008 by Amarna Publishing, Sheffield, UK

Cover illustration: Garden of a private estate with an ornamental pool, part of the wall painting from the Tomb of Nebamun, Thebes, New Kingdom, c.1350 BC (painted plaster) (British Museum, London, UK / The Bridgeman Art Library)

ISBN 978-0-9549653-1-0

Copy-editing, design and typesetting by
Mushroom Publishing, Bath, UK
mail@mushroompublishing.com

Printed and bound by
Lightning Source

To my wife for her patient support and encouragement during the writing of this book.

Contents

ACKNOWLEDGEMENTS

I am grateful to Professor Rosalie David of the KNH Centre for Biomedical Egyptology at the University of Manchester for suggesting that I should write a book about ancient Egyptian gardens and plants. I thank Jackie and John R. Campbell, who were very helpful in providing several of the photographs used in my book. They were obtained with the kind permission of The Chelsea Physic Garden, London, The Royal Botanic Gardens, Kew, London, and Professor Mohamed El Demerdash of The Medicinal Project, Sinai. I would like to thank Dr F Nigel Hepper, and the librarians at The Herbarium, Royal Botanic Gardens, Kew for helping me to select suitable books for my research. Also, the librarians at The Natural History Museum, London, The Lindley Library of The Royal Horticultural Society, London, The British Library, London and The John Rylands University Library of Manchester at Oxford Road and Deansgate. My thanks are also given to Bob Partridge, Editor of the Ancient Egypt Magazine, for providing some of the photographs. Finally I must thank Mohamed El-Hossainy El-Akkad, Supervisor General of the Ancient Egyptian Agricultural Museum, Cairo who very kindly showed me around and gave me permission to take photographs of plant remains and artefacts in the display cabinets.

FOREWORD by Kay Bellinger

Ancient Egyptian Gardens considers how the ancient Egyptians' effective management of the land led to the success of their country, in spite of having a difficult climate. Their civilisation lasted for three millennia. The great diversity of plants available to them was due not only to the indigenous plants, which covered the three terrains of the desert, Delta and Nile Valley, but to their foresight in developing and importing foreign plants. Egypt lies on the borderline between African and the Mediterranean climates; they also had access to the Middle East.

The value they held for their plants and agriculture is clear to see on the walls of temples and tombs; for example, the ceiling of a tomb belonging to a royal vintner is decorated with hanging grapes, and his wife is shown picking them. What a lovely sight for him when he awakes in the afterlife.

The importance of agriculture is obvious from the many scenes of the working countryside, painted for the dead, so when they awake they would come to life and provide sustenance. The ancient Egyptians used their plants to enhance festivals and, as today, to decorate their coffins. The land to them was of prime importance and they believed that the afterlife was just like Egypt, but better. Unlike today, the ancient Egyptians were bonded to nature.

1

AN INTRODUCTION TO EGYPT

Egypt was called *Tameri* by its people, meaning 'the beloved land'. There were other descriptive names for Egypt, such as *Ta-Akt*, meaning 'the land of flood and fertile soil', *Geb* after the name of the Earth God, and *Agypt*, meaning 'the land covered with floodwater'.

Egypt owes its existence to the Nile; the area is mainly desert except for the Nile Valley, its Delta area and a few oases. Every year the population of Ancient Egypt looked forward with anticipation to the 'inundation', which is the flooding of the low valley beside the Nile. This inundation depended upon heavy summer rains in the highlands of Ethiopia, which filled the tributaries and then the rivers Arbara, Blue Nile and White Nile. The flooding season usually started during the last week of June at Aswan and could take until September to reach the optimum level in the environs of Cairo. The flooding lasted up to four months, depending upon the amount of rainfall in Ethiopia. The height of the inundation varied from year to year; particularly high levels were experienced during the 'Middle Kingdom' period and resulted in ruined crops, loss of habitation and of the lives of peasants. An optimum level was necessary for agriculture and the livelihood of the population; it meant the difference between feast and famine. It

was also considered essential that the ritual sacrifices performed by the Pharaoh to the Gods could continue. If the flooding was meagre then the crops would suffer and be insufficient to sustain the population.

The Egyptians recognised three distinct seasons in a year which were influenced by the yearly flooding of the Nile. The Egyptian year was divided into twelve equal months, each month consisting of thirty days, plus five days at the end of the year. Each day was divided into the twelve hour day and twelve hour night. It is thought that the Babylonians were responsible for the division of the hour into sixty minutes. The Egyptian New Year occurred on the equivalent of 15th July, coinciding with the reappearance of the Dog Star called Sirius and with the beginning of the inundation at Memphis (Egypt's first capital).

The four months of the inundation was named *Akhet*. The following season, called *Peret*, began in October when the land could be cultivated ready for the sowing and planting of crops; this was the season for growing. The last four-month season was called *shemu*, when the Nile reached its lowest levels and basins and canals had dried out. *Shemu* was the time when the wheat and some other crops were harvested. The wheat grain was stored in temple warehouses, and flax, which had been left to dry in the fields, was cut down for making woven baskets after the seed heads were removed for linseed oil.

Apart from providing the water necessary to irrigate the crops, another benefit of the flooding was substantial as the fast flowing Nile brought with it beneficial silts which were deposited on the land. There was no need for fertiliser as the silts were rich in nutrients and together with the moisture in the soil encouraged rapid plant growth. The ideal level of inundation was approximately eight metres, measured by an open gauge alongside the Nile. An inundation of eight metres was considered ideal, nine would break dams and dykes, seven would provide meagre crops and six metres resulted in famine. The gauges are known as 'Nileometers' and consist of measuring steps at the water's edge that can be either entirely open or enclosed by walls. The gauges were positioned at several sites from Aswan to Alexandria in the Delta region.

During the inundation when the land could not be worked due to flooding there was very little the peasants could do on the land. In the period of the Old Kingdom (2686–2181 BC) they were hired for pyramid building. This part of the year was useful for transporting stone nearer to the construction sites by boat because of the higher water levels. The Pharaoh and his officials regarded the inundation as an important event and chose to celebrate it by the opening of the dykes and tributaries allowing distribution of the water to irrigate the land. Items such as fruit, flowers and probably food were offered to Hapy, the God who represented the Nile flood.

The officials who managed the cultivated land took measures to retain some of the flood water in man-made basins and canals for use in October and November. In October, before the land could be cultivated after flooding, overseers measured and apportioned the land to ensure that each peasant had his fair share. In some years the inundation was excessive, and in the 12th Dynasty the Pharaoh Amenemhat III sought to control it by the construction of a huge lake to store it for later use. It measured thirty miles in circumference, and was situated in the fertile valley of the Fayume about sixty miles south of Cairo and twenty-five miles to the west of the Nile. Excess water was drained into it by branches of the Bahr Yoosef Canal (Joseph's Canal) which was approximately 250 miles in length along the western border of the desert parallel with the Nile. When required, a certain amount of water could be released into a network of small canals and dykes, which spread everywhere through the arable land, allowing for balanced distribution. The lake and canal no longer exist; by the nineteenth century AD the level of inundation was much reduced, hence the need for the Aswan Dam.

In the earliest part of the growing season the requirement for watering to help the crops to flourish was minimal unless the land was further away from the Nile and at a higher level. In this case, water channelled in dykes would not reach the crops, so water was lifted by a device known as the *Shaduf*, which can still be seen in use today. The

shaduf was depicted in Theban tomb paintings. It consisted of a long bent pole on a pivot, with a clay jar at one end to hold water and a lump of clay at the other to act as a counter balance, enabling water to be lifted with minimal physical effort by the labourer. Before this device was invented labourers carried water in clay jars, sometimes with a yoke around the shoulders allowing two to be carried at a time. Much later on in the Ptolemaic period two new methods were brought to Egypt that enabled larger volumes of water to be lifted more efficiently. One of the devices was the water wheel or *sigiya*, which carried several buckets or scoops attached to it at equal intervals and was powered by oxen.

Early Egyptians using a system of weights and poles called shadufs to get water from the Nile, by Peter Jackson (1922-2003) © Look and Learn.

The other device was the Archimedes Screw. It has been postulated that the Archimedes Screw was originally a Mesopotamian invention used initially around 600 BC, or that it was an Egyptian invention. Although it is attributed to Archimedes (287–212 BC) the Greek Mathematician, physicist, and inventor, it is possible that he discovered it and improved upon it. The device consists of a long cylinder or pipe containing a screw of the same length with a turning handle at the top. The bottom end of the machine was dipped into the water source and as the screw was turned, water was scooped up into the screw. Ideally the screw machine was set at an angle and raised the water to the top of the cylinder, where it flowed into irrigation channels.

The Nile and its annual flooding is the only means by which the gardens and fields can be irrigated. Rain is very rare even in the Delta region. If heavy rain is experienced it does not last long enough to be of any benefit except in the Mediterranean coastal region.

The climate is not ideal for the growing of crops in the period between May to September even where irrigation can be provided; it is hot and dry with a typical day temperature averaging 28 degrees centigrade. It was also considered impractical to grow crops at this time due not only to the lack of water, but also to the occasional light but hot southerly winds drying out the fertile soils beside the Nile. Only established indigenous trees and plants and a few introductions to Egypt could withstand the conditions, such as the tamarisk and date-palm. Plants such as these developed extremely deep root systems in their search for water and had to be close to the Nile or oases to survive. The gardens of the Pharaohs' officials, and also temple and tomb gardens, were generally near the Nile and would have had many labourers during the summer who lifted water from the river to keep their plants alive.

In the winter period between December and February it was important to provide protection for young delicate plants as the temperature sometimes dipped below freezing point. In the early spring, strong

A hoe in the Egyptian Agricultural Museum.

cold winds can delay growth and some trees may suffer damage to leaves and branches. Later on in the spring there is a hot wind known as the *Khamsin* which usually lasts for fifty days. The heat is debilitating and can damage the flowers even of indigenous species, resulting in poor crops later on. These winds also cause dust storms which would have made it almost impossible for the garden labourers to work. It is easy to see why many of the temple and tomb gardens had walls high enough to provide shelter for both the plants and humans.

Egypt has been occupied by man since the Palaeolithic period approximately 200,000 years ago. Evidence of this is provided by the discovery of Stone Age artefacts and remains. It is suggested as a result of archaeological evidence that settled communities were established by the late sixth millennium BC in favourable areas of Egypt such as the very fertile region of the Fayum – a very large oasis with a large fresh water lake which still flourishes today as a substantial provider of food for the population of Egypt. In those days the people were to some extent still hunter gatherers (killing wild animals, fishing, gathering wild fruits, seeds and roots for food) but gradually they began to cultivate the land for the growing of cereals, vegetables and cattle. They were able to make bread from barley (*Hordeum* species) and emmer wheat (*Triticum dicoccum*) though these were selected from wild species and their yield was poor. It was not until the Late Period, between 1035 and 332 BC, sometimes known as the decline of Pharaonic rule, when the much higher-yielding wheat was introduced.

The Early Dynastic Period (Old Kingdom) began around 3100 BC when Upper and Lower Egypt was unified under the rule of Narmer (Menes). According to the Greek historian Herodotus, Narmer was the king who first established the capital city of Memphis, though he needed to reclaim land by damming the Nile. The earliest writing appeared at this time, as evidenced by the Narmer palette which can be seen in the Egyptian Museum in Cairo. This slate palette is carved in relief and it is notable that both sides show the earliest found form of hieroglyphic writing. According to the author of *Ancient Egyptian*

Medicine, John F. Nunn, Egypt began trading with Lebanon in the Second Dynasty for the supply of wood and certain drugs.

There is evidence to suggest that the environment of Pharaonic Egypt differed to some degree from the environment of the present day, especially with regard to the extent of vegetation. It is known that forests were well established in the Sahara region west of the Nile valley during the last wet period, according to Alessandra Nibbi. Her research covered the areas of Hoggar and Tibesti in the Saharan highlands. In the Neolithic period, and possibly earlier, this area featured forests of oak and cedar and associated plants that were typical of the Mediterranean region, which normally has hot dry summers and winter rain. This type of vegetation survived for a long time after the Quaternary wet period had ended. Despite the drying out of this region there are a few very small areas where stunted remains can be found. In Neolithic times the oak and cedar forests died out gradually as the typical Mediterranean vegetation became dominant, such as Jerusalem pine, juniper cypress, olive, myrtle and common fig. Later, probably due to winter rains becoming less frequent or less reliable, savannah vegetation took over from the Mediterranean vegetation. Savannah is a land sparsely covered with low vegetation, particularly grasses and shrubs which can appear to be dead during long periods of drought, and were often treeless or dotted with trees or patches of wood as in tropical or sub-tropical Africa. This process of change continues, resulting in the total degradation of regions, which become arid and dry desert, and overgrazing and deforestation can often be a factor.

There is some dispute about the ability of the Egyptian Pharaonic period to provide most of its own needs for timber, such as Cedar of Lebanon (*Cedrus libani*), Jerusalem Pine (*Pinus halepensis*) and Juniper (species unknown). Research by various experts, such as Alessandra Nibbi, Quézel and Martine Rossignol, suggests that forests existed on the borders of Egypt, in the Sahara west of the Nile, and in the delta region of Northern Egypt. Since Pharaonic times the desert has increased in area. Core samples taken at various Egyptian sites showed

the remains of pollen grains. A sufficient quantity of pollen was found in the Nile Delta near Rosetta to prove that Jerusalem pine (*Pinus halepensis*) grew there.

2

THE BEGINNINGS OF
THE FORMAL GARDEN

Egyptian Gardens

The Egyptian garden in history was mainly formal in design, and our knowledge of them is drawn from representations in tomb paintings, sometimes from plans drawn on paving slabs, and sometimes in the form of wooden models, such as the one in the Egyptian Museum in Cairo. These early gardens were the forerunners of formal Moorish gardens, such as the Alhambra in Spain, formal Persian gardens, which are represented on some of their hand-woven carpets, and even formal Elizabethan gardens.

The ancient gardens of Egypt were often situated near water sources and usually on raised ground to avoid flooding from the Nile. Shade was an essential requirement as the summers in Egypt are extremely hot and dry, and was usually provided by date palms and other trees, which only flourish by the river or another water source such as a canal or oasis. The gardens were surrounded by high mud-brick walls which were necessary to keep out animals, to protect the garden from strong

winds, and to reduce the effect of sand storms. Private tomb gardens for the Pharaohs and officials also needed walls for privacy and security.

Methen, Governor of the Northern Delta District in Egypt during the reign of Sneferu (*circa* 2600–2576 BC — the 4th Dynasty) described a garden on the walls of his tomb. His garden extended to approximately one hectare, and there was also a vineyard of more than 405 hectares that would have produced a huge quantity of wine. The garden had a very large lake and contained a house measuring 200 cubits by 200 cubits (a cubit is equivalent to approximately half a metre) that was surrounded by some fine trees including figs.

Many important officials had large houses with gardens attached which were set out in a formal style with a pool and external walls to protect the garden. Egyptians were fond of flowers and shade trees. Gardens are mentioned throughout the history of Egypt, frequently belonging to temples and private houses. Private individuals living in towns where space was limited often chose to build their houses around shade providing trees, giving the appearance that they had been planted

An ancient Egyptian garden (engraving). The Stapleton Collection.

in the courtyard of the house. Nebamun, a police captain of King Tuthmosis IV (*c*.1405 BC) had the same idea for his Theban residence. A painting in his tomb shows two palm trees overshadowing and appearing as if they come from the centre of the house, which would have been built of mud brick and coloured with a pink wash.

The first record of a tomb garden comes from a woodcarving found buried in the tomb of Meketre, Chancellor to King Mentuhotep II (*c*.2000 BC). A model in Cairo Museum is a representation of the one found in the tomb. The original was carved in wood and painted green and shows a high walled garden with a fish pond in the centre surrounded by sycomore fig trees (*Ficus sycomorus*, a fig tree common in Egypt with leaves resembling those of the mulberry) to provide shade. At one end there is an entrance to the house and garden, and in front of it are pillars carved to resemble stems of the papyrus (*Cyperus papyrus*).

It is not known whether the tomb paintings are representative of real gardens, or are symbolic of a belief that they provided refreshment for the soul on its journey in the world of the dead or afterlife. Egyptians imagined that they could be seated in the shade of

Model of the villa and garden of Meketre.

15

a beautiful fruiting tree and the Goddess would welcome them with water and fruit from the tree to replenish them. It is important to recognise that the storage of the dead Pharaoh in a tomb was so that his soul (Ba) could return in the after-life and be rejuvenated by the wall scenes. These wall paintings featured many activities that he enjoyed and appreciated during his lifetime. It was common practise for his relatives to leave offerings such as food for his consumption and flowers for his pleasure in the tomb daily. Farmers of their land were expected to give a proportion of their produce to provide for offerings needed in the tomb of the Pharaohs. An artefact that was recovered known as the Turin Papyrus actually had illustrations which almost went as far as to show the sexual act.

Percy Withers, in *Egypt of Yesterday and Today*, wrote of Sennufer, the Overseer of the gardens of Amun under Amenophis II (1460 BC) at Thebes:

> *How fitting that his body should rest for ever under a canopy of the vine! The long stems and tendrils were inter-twined without any thought for uniform adjustment yet they are so contrived as to leave no ugly spaces on the white surface, and great purple bunches of fruit are freely distributed among the brown clustering branches. Only a people with joy in their heart could have devised such decoration for the roof of a tomb.*
>
> Percy Withers, *Egypt of Yesterday and Today*, pp.120/121

In the tomb at Thebes of Nebamun, an 18th Dynasty accountant whose responsibility was managing the granaries of Egypt, is a painting (*c*.1380 BC) on one of the walls of a private garden. The garden featured a large pond in the centre containing lotus flowers, fish, ducks and geese. Banks of black mud containing mixed herbaceous plants surround the pond. The bordering trees that can be identified in the garden are Common Fig (*Ficus carica*), Sycomore Fig (*Ficus sycomorus*), date–palm (*Phoenix dactylifera*) and doum–palm (*Hyphaene thebaica*). In

the shade of the trees is a large mandrake (*Mandragora officinarum*) which is full of fruit, and an unsupported vine in the left corner. Coming out of the shade of the trees is Hathor, the sycomore goddess who will supply the needs of Nebamun in the afterlife.

Nebamun's private garden. Part of the wall painting from the Tomb of Nebamun, Thebes, New Kingdom, *c.*1350 BC (painted plaster). Egyptian 18th Dynasty. British Museum, London.

Ineni, the architect employed to supervise the building projects of King Tuthmosis I (1528–1510 BC) built for himself a residence with a large garden that had an impressive number of trees. The wall painting in Ineni's tomb at Thebes (No.81) shows a view of the house with the fishpond and garden behind.

The wall painter did not show every tree that is listed in the complete inventory of trees and plants written in hieroglyphs above the painting. According to the inventory, the orchard contained the following:

73 sycomore fig trees; 31 persea (*Mimusops laurifolia*) trees; 170 date-palms (*Phoenix dactylifera*); 120 doum-palms (*Hyphaene thebaica*); 5 fig trees (*Ficus carica*); 2 moringa (*Moringa peregrina*) trees; 12 grape vines (*Vitis vinifera*); 5 pomegranate tree (*Punica granatum*); 16 carob trees (*Ceratonia siliqua*); 5 Christ's-thorn (*Zisiphus spina-christi*); 1 argun-palm (*Medemia argun*); 8 willow trees (*Salix subserrata*); 10 tamarisk trees (*Tamarix articulata* and *nilotica*); 5 twn trees (possibly a species of acacia); 2 myrtle (*Myrtus communis L.*) and 5 unidentified kinds of tree.

The most interesting Egyptian illustration of a garden is perhaps that from the tomb of Sennufer, a general of Amenophis III (*c.*1500 BC) at Thebes. The illustration shows a garden surrounded by a wall. The River Nile runs past the right hand side of the garden, providing the water for the garden. On the inside of the wall bordering the river is an avenue of date-palms providing necessary shade. The garden is entered by a high entrance door and archway covered with hieroglyphs. In the centre are grapevines, enclosed by a wall, and they are trained on timber pillars and rafters providing shade for the paved area beneath. There are four rectangular ponds surrounding the vineyard of the garden which are fringed by Papyrus and contain Lotus Lilies (*Nymphaea lotus*). Ducks are shown swimming on the water, and beside the two ponds nearest the house there are two shelters with a seat where the owner can enjoy the garden under cover (described as kiosks). The inside of the outer walls were bordered by date and doum-palms (identified by their split trunks) planted alternately with conical trees which

might have been sycamore figs. On the far side of the vineyard is a three-storey house and on the other side is an avenue of trees.

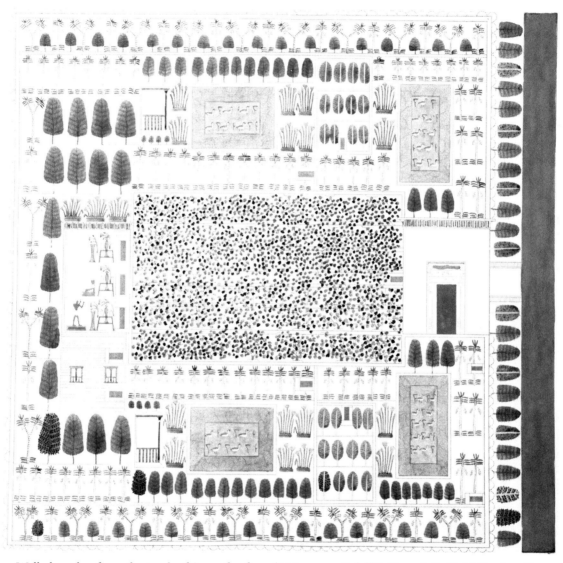

Walled garden from the tomb of Sennufer, from 'I Monumenti dell'Egitto e della Nubia' by Ippolito Rossellini (1800–43), published 1834. The Stapleton Collection.

The early temple garden excavated at Queen Hatshepsut's temple at Deir el-Bahri reveals trees planted in rows beside the ramp leading to the entrance. The tree pits or planting holes show that there were three avenues, each having seven sycamore figs and tamarisk trees planted alternately. Statues of King Mentuhotep II (Nebhepetra) (11th Dynasty 2061–2010 BC) were shaded by the sycamore figs and there was evidence of separate geometric flowerbeds. Also uncovered during excavations were the remaining roots of *Mimusops laurifolia* which must have been planted at a later date in avenues alongside the approach to Queen Hatshepsut's terraced temple.

Work on Queen Hatshepsut's temple began in the sixth or seventh year of her reign, and carried on until the twentieth year of her reign. It was never completed. Senenmut, who was described as 'Overseer' of the gardens, directed construction of the gardens. During the same period Queen Hatshepsut brought incense trees, resin, tusks and other products from Punt. However, the incense trees did not survive, probably through lack of water.

The trees that are often illustrated growing in gardens are date-palm and doum-palm, sycamore figs, pomegranate, olive, vine and willow. Trees were arranged in straight rows, usually of one particular species. In the tomb of Amenemhat Mahu (Theban Tomb 85) the innermost row was of sycamore figs, the middle row was of alternating date and doum-palms, and trees with spreading branches stood in the outermost row. Trees were very important in Egyptian landscapes and were planted in avenues in front of temples, and surrounded the gardens to provide a windbreak. Besides those trees already mentioned, excavations have shown that tamarisk, cedars and mimusops also grew on sacred sites.

It is rather odd that very few paintings of gardens have yet been discovered on the walls of Pharaoh's tombs. However, there is a carved ivory panel on the lid of a casket from the tomb of King Tutankhamun (18th Dynasty) in the Egyptian Museum at Cairo. The picture carved into the lid shows Tutankhamun and his Queen represented in what

appears to be a garden. The Queen is presenting two magnificent bouquets to the King consisting of lotus, papyrus and poppies. Behind the King is a kiosk decorated with flowers, and the picture is bordered by a frieze of cornflower, mandrake and poppies. Also on the lid, below the scene, is a picture of two children picking mandrakes and poppies — they are thought to be members of the family. The front panel features the King seated beside a fishpond with the Queen at his feet, and in his hands is a bow and arrow aimed at birds or fish within a garden.

In ancient Egypt the Pharaohs were thought to be selected to rule over their people by divine right of the gods. The temples were dedicated to both the gods and the pharaohs and the sacred gardens had a role in their worship. The gods and the kings were regarded as the givers and preservers of life, therefore vegetation and fertility provided by plants and trees were important.

The temple garden of Mentuhotep II at Deir el-Bahri is said to be the earliest site where there is any accurate evidence of tree planting at a mortuary temple (c.2020 BC). An aerial view above the temple complex clearly shows circular depressions or pits on both sides of the ramp leading to the temple. Fourteen of the pits nearest to the temple were excavated and contained the remains of roots, leaves and bark of sycamore fig and tamarisk trees. The pits were surprisingly deep, which suggests that the trees had substantial root systems. The remaining pits had no traces of roots, indicating that the planting of further trees was not completed. Apart from the remains of the tree pits, one of the paving slabs in the temple had part of a plan of the site sketched on it, perhaps done by the landscape architect.

South of the ramp facing the temple and in between the row of trees were remains of stems and roots of flowering plants contained in two substantially sized beds. There were rows of tamarisk trees directly in front of the mortuary temple, spaced at regular intervals and planted in pits 2.4 metres wide and 1.3 metres deep.

The sycomore and tamarisk were chosen for symbolic and religious reasons. Hathor, the sky goddess, dwelling in the sycomore, consumed

the sun every night, and the soul of the god Osiris rested in the tamarisk. Also, in the same tree, the pharaoh (in this case Mentuhotep II) was believed to be reborn with the sun every morning.

Overview of Mentuhotep's Temple.

Adjacent to the temple of Mentuhotep II is the terraced temple of Queen Hatshepsut, completed circa 1470 BC, and it also had remains of gardens. The garden in the outer court had circular planting pits enclosing two T-shaped pools either side of the central ramp. In the bottom of the pools, deposits of dried Nile mud remained which on analysis showed that they were planted with papyrus.

At Tel-el-Amarna, a city in Middle Egypt built by Akhenaten and Nefertiti (c.1367–1350 BC) there were several gardens found during excavations. Also, several rooms of houses were uncovered with their walls painted with representations of plants, birds and water beasts, giving the illusion of looking out onto courtyards and pools.

Akhenaten, otherwise known as Amenophis II, was one of the greatest Egyptian garden architects. The city of Amarna had several parks and gardens, despite being in a remote part of the desert vulnerable to hot, drying winds in the summer and freezing nights in the winter. It would not have been easy to establish plants and trees in the poor dry soil without digging pits and surrounding the roots with enough alluvial fertile mud to hold moisture and nutrients. As the city was next to the Nile the area would have benefited from the annual inundation and water could be obtained at other times, but large quantities would have been needed to keep the trees alive and allow them to establish.

The plants and trees required for this huge project probably came from other royal gardens some considerable distance away, and were transported by boat along the River Nile.

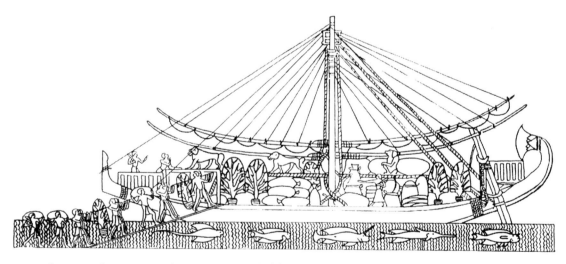

Loading myrrh trees on a ship in Punt; a relief from Queen Hatshepsut's temple at Deir el-Bahri.

The Egyptians are thought to have been capable of transporting large trees. Queen Hatshepsut imported incense trees from Punt for her temple at Deir el-Bahri. However, date palms are not easy to transport because the growing point is quite brittle and easily broken. The main method of reproduction is from suckers taken from mature trees, and this allows trees of the right sex to be selected, ensuring pollination and date fruit production. Small trees and plants would have been much easier to transport, and also easier to transplant and so more likely to establish in their new site. But it would have taken several years before any of the fruiting trees were able to produce fruit. Given the right growing conditions, grape vines (*Vitis vinifera*) take up to 3 years to fruit, common figs (*Ficus carica*) and sycamore-figs (*Ficus sycamorus*) 2 to 3 years, and olives (*Olea europaca*) 6 years, all from cuttings.

Akhenaten's gardens had a number of pools which would have been easily stocked with the water plants growing in the Nile and a nearby canal, such as water lilies (Lotus), papyrus and reeds.

The large gardens Akhenaten built in the southern part of Amarna featured several garden pavilions, and his most important courtiers built a few in their private gardens. The garden pavilion became an important feature in Egypt and was copied by the Islamic Kingdoms.

Akhenaten considered that gardens, plants and trees were an important feature of temple and tomb buildings. Many of the building walls

Painted pavement from The Great Palace complex at Amarna.

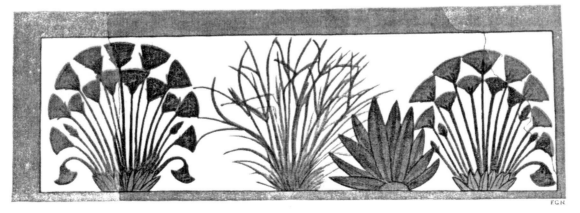

were covered with paintings of palm trees, vines bearing grapes, and exotic flowering plants. The walls were particularly bright and colourfully painted on the outside as well as on the inside, some showing the King and Queen offering fruits and other products from the garden as part of their worship of the Aten. Excavations also revealed that some garden walls were covered by coloured tiles illustrating flowering plants and palm trees. Even the pavement was painted with illustrations of plants and trees.

So why was there a desire to illustrate the walls to such an extent? Perhaps the King wanted to imagine the gardens when they were mature. Also, he wished to provide a paradise for the God Aten. Amarna was such a newly created city that it would be several years before the trees and plants were large enough to appear well-established.

Many of the plants illustrated on the walls and floors were typical of those that could be found growing in the favourable areas of Egypt. The water plants included were the *Cyperus* species — *C. alopecuroides*, *C. esculentus* and *C. rotundus* — and *Arundo donax*, white and blue lotus, and *Phragmites australis*. Fruit trees included date-palms, sycamore figs, common figs, grapes and olives. Flowering plants included poppy, cornflower, mandrake, *chrysanthemum coronarium*, and plants of the hollyhock family that grew naturally on land close to the Nile. The indigenous flowers were probably cultivated as offerings to the Aten, and for other ceremonial purposes.

Huge quantities of food would have been needed to feed the large population required to support the court of the Pharaoh, which in Amarna lasted for fourteen years. Possibly hundreds of garden labourers were required to cultivate the land and grow the crops that provided vegetables, grains, wine and oils for cooking and other purposes. A substantial quantity of grain, meat, and wine was not produced locally and Amarna depended upon Thebes to provide its main supplies. Thebes

Painted pavement from The Great Palace complex at Amarna.

was the capital of the previous Pharaohs and all the important people had moved from there to Amarna. The lands around Thebes continued to provide products for Amarna and were still managed by landowners and bailiffs of the King, and taxes were levied on these supplies.

In Amarna, excavations provide evidence of walled parks which served as sacred areas for the worship of the Aten and for the King to display his divinity to the people. Various ceremonies may have taken place, such as the celebration of the New Year and the arrival of the annual inundation. Two parks have been found, one about 5 km south of the city, called the Maru-Aten, and the other one 3 km north of the city centre, called the Northern Maru.

The Maru-Aten consisted of two walled garden enclosures; the Northern one nearer to the city was much larger than the one adjacent to it on the south side. The outer walls were strengthened by buttresses, and

paintings of grape vines and swags of flowers decorated them. The enclosures were accessed by a columned Entrance Hall in the southern wall. From recent excavations it is thought that the northern enclosure was built later. The entrance to the southern enclosure led along a path past an ornamental pool and through a gateway into the northern enclosure.

In the centre of the northern enclosure was a lake measuring 120 metres long by 60 metres wide by 1 metre deep, shaped like a cartouche.

The lake took up approximately one third of the enclosure, which also contained several buildings, temples, offering pools, and, of course, flowers and trees.

A main road led from the city to the entrance, which was a pavilion or hall with a series of columns to represent palms. The walls were decorated with paintings depicting the King in procession and his subjects paying their respects. Another scene shows Akhenaten with his family stretching out their hands to touch papyrus bouquets and offering them in order to give their blessings to the Aten. Looking east into the southern enclosure from the pavilion was a garden containing shrubs and trees, and at the far side near to the wall there was another building.

On the west side of the lake a pier goes part way towards the centre with steps down into the water at the end. The pier ran west to east, and half way along its length on the land were steps which led down onto ground that was divided into garden plots.

Just before the steps into the water there was a stone gateway carved in relief showing the Aten being worshipped by the King. Also, in front of a temple entrance, running soldiers were depicted with their prisoners, and servants or priests bringing bouquets of papyrus as offerings. There is the remains of a temple opposite the pier on the east side of the Lake — perhaps they were meant to be bowing to this. The King was probably rowed across the lake to the temple in a ceremonial boat.

Lakes were a feature of Egyptian temple complexes and regarded as symbolic of the creation of life on earth represented by the God Nun of the primeval water. In the case of Amarna and the Maru-Aten, the King took the place of the god.

A Maru was a sacred place dedicated to the sun-god Aten who was revered by King Akhenaten. Ceremonies took place to celebrate the annual inundation. The nearby city of Amarna was where the Aten was formed and according to one of the creation myths this mound was where he might rest away from the primeval waters. It was also a resting place for the solar boat after it had made its daily journey through the heavens.

By the sight of your rays all flowers exist
What lives and sprouts from the soil grows when you shine
Drinking deep of your sight all flocks frisk.

Short Hymn to the Aten (Lichtheim, *p.92*)

In other words, the Aten represented the sun's rays that provided life for all creation, and in whose light all creatures and plants thrive.

About three kilometres north of the centre of the city of Amarna was a complex now known as the 'Northern Maru' which, although it was much smaller, was similar in layout to the 'Maru-Aten'. Near the central pool was a sunken garden enclosed by buildings having several small rooms with openings facing towards it. Steps led down into the garden which was divided into small rectangular flower beds watered by a channel running underneath the building and connected to the central pool, the water being supplied from the Nile. One of the rooms in the complex of buildings, with a view through to the central pool, may have been dedicated to Meritaten, eldest daughter of Akhenaten and Nefertiti. Her name was inscribed on the door posts, and it is thought that she may have contributed to the design of the gardens on this site.

Besides the marus, there was a ceremonial area in the centre of Amarna which included a great temple and a royal palace. On the south side of the palace were two sunken gardens on either side of a central building that may have been used for ceremonial purposes. Sir Flinders Petrie, who was involved with the excavations, named them the northern and southern 'harems of the palace'. The Northern Sunken Garden in some ways resembles a Roman Atrium, as it is within a colonnaded court with a garden in the centre. The terraced garden measured 20 metres long by 10 metres wide and had four raised beds, possibly for flowering plants, along the length of the sunken area. At a lower level, shade trees were planted in pits to provide shade from the exceedingly hot sun. Water for the trees and plants was provided by a channel connected to a well and a water tank. The drawing shows one part of the

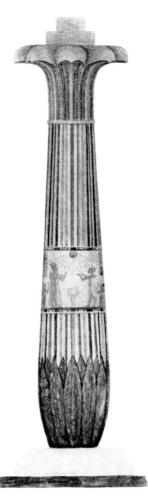

Painted column from
the Maru-Aten.

28

colonnade supported by wooden pillars, which might have been strong enough to support a flat roof.

The colonnaded building around the garden shows evidence that the walls were painted in an elaborate fashion. One wall features water

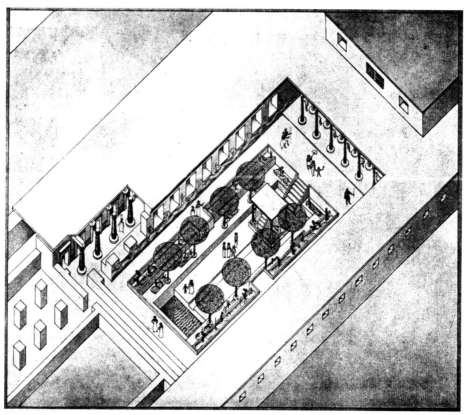

Great Palace — isometric drawing of the North Harem restored.

lilies, while others feature grapes piled up on offering dishes, and many other scenes relating to life in the region are depicted. The rest of the columns were made of stone and were tiled. The tiles had a shiny glazed surface now known as 'Faience', a ceramic tile which the Egyptians first started producing from the Old Kingdom onwards. Various patterns could be applied or moulded to the base material of the tile, to which

29

the glazing material was added. They were then fired to a high temperature giving the tile a hard finish. The image or design within the glaze appeared in relief, and in this case the columns were decorated with tiles made to represent bundles of papyrus, and the capitals of the columns to resemble the flowers (umbels).

Assyrian Gardens

Mesopotamia (now a part of Iraq) was a country that is very similar to Egypt in that it has a delta area which is very fertile. It is supplied by the rivers Tigris and Euphrates and before the land was settled by the Sumerian tribes it was mainly swamp that only grew a giant reed, *Phragmites australis*. The Sumerians arrived in the area before 3000 BC and constructed canals to drain the swamps and to supply irrigation to the desert areas alongside the canals, as in Egypt. The Euphrates and Tigris flooded the delta area and part of the plains annually, like the Nile.

To the west of the lower Euphrates the ancient royal city of Ur became established, possibly due to the fertility of the area. It is thought that fruit trees and vegetables were grown within the inner and outer fortifications of the city walls.

Penelope Hobhouse, in her book *Plants in Garden History* (*p.16*) says that: "A fable of the time relates how a king planted a date palm and a tamarisk in the courtyard of his palace and held a banquet in the shade of the tamarisk. An early Babylonian text proclaims 'I planted a pure orchard for the goddess and established fruit deliveries as regular offerings.'"

In the tenth century BC the Assyrians who originally came from the northern plains of Asia were warring invaders and gradually became dominant in most of Western Asia. Later, by the fourth century BC, their empire had extended to Palestine and Egypt. It is perhaps significant that, just like in Egypt, sacred temples had trees planted around them. Although the rites that took place beneath them were a little different, they may have based these layouts on the Egyptian temples. Penelope Hobhouse says that "although archaeologists have found few traces of inner palace gardens it is thought that the Assyrian Kings probably had private courtyards to which they could retreat, where palms, pines and fruit trees provided shade; these were almost certainly laid out in a geometric pattern." (*Plants in Garden History, p.17*).

The Assyrians illustrated many aspects of their lives in palaces and temples, carved in bas-relief on stone built walls. They depicted single storey houses which appear to have their foundations raised above ground level to reduce the possibility of flooding. Also they show roof gardens with flowers and even trees growing on them, and the water provided by lifting it from the river nearby. A site excavated where the first Assyrian capital of Assur was established revealed what appears to be a formal garden with several flower beds in the centre of an inner court with several beds arranged outside of it. It is thought that royal gardens were designed in a similar fashion, and that flowers were grown for offerings to the Gods.

Babylonian Gardens

By the end of the seventh century BC the dominance of the Assyrians declined due to attacks from the warring tribes of Scythians, Medians and Babylonians who combined to destroy the Assyrian empire. The later Assyrian capital of Nineveh was destroyed along with its gardens, the only evidence is the remaining ruined mounds. Nebuchadnezzar II (605–562 BC) the grandson of the leading Babylonian warrior, Nabopolassar, created the capital of Babylon and became famous for constructing the Hanging Gardens beside the Euphrates. It is claimed that the gardens were created for Nebuchadnezzar's new wife, Amytis.

The Hanging Gardens of Babylon, from a series of the 'Seven Wonders of the World' published in 'Munchener Bilderbogen', 1886 by Knab, Ferdinand (1834-1902) (Archives Charmet).

33

Being a native of Media she was used to a cooler climate where trees and plants probably flourished among the hills and meadows.

This huge construction built in the hot, arid desert was discovered in a state of decay by the Romans some five hundred years later. Historians of the time described it as several layers of terrace built on top of each other in a pyramidal fashion, with a total area of 1.4 hectares (35 acres). Constructed of baked bricks, the terraces appeared to have been waterproofed with stone slabs and layers of reed. The terraces supported earth and many trees closely planted, possibly watered by a complex hydraulic watering system known as the Archimedes screw, which would have allowed them to flourish. Considering the large quantity of water required to irrigate such a large area, it would have been impossible to have watered them using clay pots carried by labourers. The Archimedes screw has a winding handle that had to be turned manually but would lift much larger amounts in a much shorter time and for less manpower. The Hanging Gardens of Babylon is one of the Seven Wonders of the World, and it is difficult to imagine how substantial it must have been. The foundations and supports for such a construction must have been immensely strong, possibly built directly onto rock. Many of the trees would have been planted to provide shade and could have included date palms, cedars, evergreen oaks, pines, pomegranates, olives and tamarisk. The Assyrians imported many flowering plants from the north and west and it is quite likely that the Babylonians did the same. If so they may have consisted of jasmine, roses, Madonna lily, tulips and poppies.

Persian Gardens

The land to the east of Mesopotamia known as Persia (now Iran) was occupied by the Medians and Achaemenians during the ninth to the fourth centuries. They developed garden enclosures or parks which the Persians called 'pairidaeza' translated as 'pardes' in Hebrew. When the Greeks first translated the Bible the enclosures became known as 'paradeisos' and in English the word became 'paradise'. The Persians' paradise gardens probably included a palace or pavilion and were planted with trees and orchards, watered by some form of irrigation system.

In the Christian tradition "The Garden of Eden" (Genesis 1) as described in the Bible is an earthly paradise; a Heaven on earth created by God which, because man sinned, became unobtainable. This may be a myth, but man, it seems, has ever since strived to re-create the Garden of Paradise.

In the Islamic tradition the garden is regarded symbolically as a paradise, with shade and water being a very important part of it. Gardens beside running water are blissful for the soul, places where there is time for quiet reflection. The symmetrically quartered gardens were divided by four channels which met in the centre, and the gardens, contained within a walled enclosure, were known as 'Chahar Bagh'.

The Persians were the originators of the Chahar Bagh 2500 years ago and the design was adopted later by the Islamic tradition. In fact, Cyrus the Great is acknowledged as introducing this design or concept in his royal Pasargadae palace garden (see below).

The early Islamic idea of a paradise garden was that it should contain within its walls fruit trees, water and pavilions where the wealthy or privileged could relax in the shade. Many of these gardens were surrounded by desert, a stark contrast to the luxuriant green growth found in a garden oasis.

The Classical Greeks spoke of large walled areas or parks planted

with trees and cover for animals, called 'paradeisos', where the Persian Kings could go hunting in peace away from the gaze of their subjects.

Astyages gave his grandson Cyrus the Great 'all the game present in the paradeisos' at this time so that he could learn to hunt (Xenophon, *Cyropaedia* 1.3.14, 8.1.34–8).

Persia was conveniently placed to be influenced by the trade routes which passed through their country and could obtain silk from China, spice from India and salt from Arabia. There would also be an exchange of ideas and it is quite likely they would have heard of the developments in the architecture of buildings and gardens in the west and the east. In particular it is almost certain they would know about the temples and gardens of Egypt and their expertise in growing crops for food.

Archaeologists have excavated the sites of two Achaemenian palaces at Pasargadae and Persepolis and found evidence of narrow irrigation channels which could have watered trees or plants. The remains of the palace at Pasargadae near Isfahan, built for Cyrus the Great in the sixth century BC, include a fifth century columned Audience Hall and a garden pavilion within a rectangular walled garden. The buildings were linked to a series of gravity-fed stone channels, which opened out into pools at set intervals. It is likely that these channels were capable of carrying water to flower beds and avenues of trees inside the outer walls.

Excavations in the 1960's revealed the design of the gardens surrounding the palace of Cyrus the Great (559–530 BC). An inner garden or court measuring 230 by 200 metres

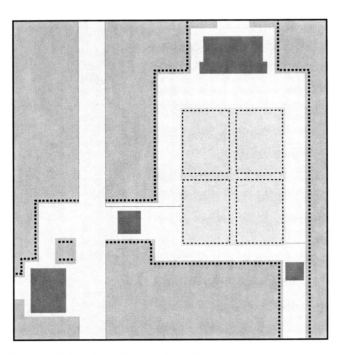

The quadripartite palace garden at Pasargadae — a typical example of a Chahar Bagh.

was surrounded by a wide path and divided into four equal plots with stone watercourses around each one.

The King, sitting in the palace, could look down the centre of the garden from the portico, and possibly onto a vista beyond. This inner court was enclosed by a row of trees on four sides which could only be reached via a gate, by crossing a bridge and passing through a garden pavilion.

Although the palace sites were established in hot and arid desert areas, the irrigation systems adopted would have allowed trees and plants to flourish. "The Achaemenians were also responsible for expanding the existing underground watering system, the *qanats*, which although superseded today by mechanised wells and large-scale dams (if not damaged by conquerors from the east during the Middle Ages or running dry through changes in the water level), can still provide essential water for crops and gardens." (Penelope Hobhouse, *Plants in Garden History*, p.19)

The mountains were the source of plentiful supplies of water when the snow melted in the spring. This created possibly thousands of fast flowing streams running into ever-larger rivers. Due to the heat of the desert most of the streams and rivers dried up before they reached the sea so man could not depend on this source for long. In order to obtain a more reliable supply of water the Achaemenians and earlier tribes of Persian people dug shafts down to the constant subterranean water table usually found at the base of mountains surrounding the Iranian plateau. These were known as Qanats, and could vary in length from a few metres to many kilometres, gradually going down hill to where the water was required. Having found water by digging the first shaft, a second one was dug lower down the slope. Its base was lower than the first shaft allowing sufficient gradient for the water to run down when the excavated tunnel joined the two shafts. Along the course of the tunnel a vertical shaft was dug every 15 metres or so to allow air supply for the workers and to allow dispersal of excavated material. The shafts were kept open allowing maintenance of the qanats. In some

parts, where the ground was porous, the channels were lined with stone or tile. These qanats can still be seen and it is not unusual to see two or three or more qanat channels running parallel to each other in the desert. Many of them are dried up and no longer in use due to a great increase in the use of water by industry and a great expansion of the population.

Where the water emerged from the qanats it ran into open water channels whereupon the owner or his lessee could stake claim to the water for his own use. Water could then be directed into a collecting tank or pool and from there be used for irrigation of his crops.

Typically the fields were divided up into a grid pattern of shallow channels made of mud reinforced with brushwood. The walls of these channels could be broken or re-sealed as and when necessary to allow flooding of the plot to water the crop. Any remaining water was collected in a catchment pool or reservoir for later use. The grid system adopted is very similar to the method used in Ancient Egypt for irrigating crops. However, the Persians had the benefit of constant gravity fed water using the system of qanats.

The qanats were important for the supply of drinking water to the people living in the villages on the high Iranian plateau. It is probable that this system supplied the palaces of Pasargadae and Persepolis and their gardens allowing trees and flowers to thrive. The Persians, in an effort to improve agriculture, enlarged and repaired the canal system that the Sumerians established in the low plains between the Tigris and the Euphrates. However, as in Egypt, the supply of water was plentiful only for a few months, in this case due to the melting of the snow in the mountains, and it sometimes caused flooding of the plains.

Gradually the Persian empire expanded west, capturing Nebuchadnezzar's capital of Babylon in 538 BC, and eventually reaching the borders of Egypt and overrunning all the countries of their known world.

The Persian garden was featured in their art and design and represented on interior walls of palaces in the form of mosaics and paintings.

The same designs could be found on ceramics, and on carpets in particular, where the Chahar Bagh was sometimes featured. The pattern might consist of an octagonal pool or pavilion in the centre with motifs of plants and trees in the central panel and geometric motifs around the borders. Gardens in Persia were not confined to the surrounds of Royal palaces and parks; it was quite common for old Iranian town houses to have gardens within their plain mud brick walls. If there was not a garden the houses would have a courtyard containing a Palm Tree or two to provide shade just as in ancient Egypt, a basic design that still exists in the Middle East today.

Greek Gardens

Alexander the Great conquered Persia, and although he destroyed Darius' Persepolis in 330 BC, he brought Greek culture to this area and adopted the Royal Parks of the Persian Kings. He is said to have returned to the royal park in Babylon where he bathed and rested for a little while before he died in 323 BC. Alexander's treasurer Harpalos was responsible for the royal gardens at Babylon. He introduced Greek plants that were able to withstand the hot climate of the Persian Gulf, though the ivy he tried failed to flourish. Alexander the Great's successors established Greek Kingdoms in Macedonia, Asia Minor, Syria and Egypt. It was fashionable for the Roman upper classes to have wall paintings in Roman houses illustrating the royal gardens and game parks of the Persian or Hellenistic Greek Kings.

In the fifth and fourth centuries BC, Greece was a democratic society and so Royal Parks were unknown until they discovered them in Persia. Information about Greek gardens, either ornamental or utilitarian, is nonexistent before the eighth century BC; it is not until the fifth century BC that there is evidence of gardens of any sort.

The Greek parks were known as 'gymnasia' and three were established in the suburbs of Athens where plentiful supplies of water could be obtained from the Kephissos, Eridanos and Ilissos rivers. They were established in Academy, Lykeion and Kynosarges and sited within ancient sacred groves where religious events took place.

The philosophers Plato, Aristotle, Theophrastus and Epicurus established schools of their own in the wooded areas near the gymnasia. The gardens were sited next to the houses of the philosophers and though on a smaller scale they were similar in design to the larger gymnasium parks. Within the grounds of the philosopher Theophrastus, where he had a colonnade and a garden for the muses (a Mouseion), the philosopher practised his own funerary cult. When he died the garden was bequeathed to his friends to enable them to study literature and

philosophy there. The aristocratic Romans' villas were based on the same ideas as the Greek philosophers' gardens. Cicero established a gymnasium at his villa near Tusculum in the first century, which featured Greek works of art including herms (squared pillars surmounted by a head or bust, usually of Hermes) and a statue of Plato. He called it his 'Academy'. Because of the advice and close friendship he had with Titus Pomponius (who received the cognomen 'Atticus') he considered it should be given to him.

The cities and towns of ancient Greece were built within the confines of defensive walls, and individual housing was very densely packed together leaving no room for gardens. In the suburbs and rural areas next to rivers and streams, water was available to gardens for growing fruit, flowers and vegetables. Also there were a few large estates further away in the country growing grain, grapes and fruit on a larger scale. According to the literature of the time, gardens were regarded as a luxury. Evidence from the fourth century BC indicates that Plato purchased a garden in the suburbs of Athens for 2000 drachmas in 388 BC, and that Epicurus paid 8000 drachmas for his garden. To be able to purchase property of this value you would be classed as very wealthy — a labourer in Athens earned on average only one drachma per day.

Alexander the Great established the city of Alexandria in the late fourth century BC but space was still limited for the majority of housing. Some houses, probably belonging to the more important citizens, had a courtyard in the centre with covered walkways supported by stone columns (peristyles). The courtyard was open to the air and generally paved, sometimes with mosaics, but there is no evidence that gardens were cultivated in these areas. King Ptolemy and his dynasty built palaces surrounded by planted areas even within the city of Alexandria. In the suburbs, the Ptolomaic kings established palaces, groves and parks which although built in the Hellenistic period followed the traditional architecture of the ancient Pharaonic period.

Roman Gardens

The Romans seemed to have a different outlook. They saw gardens as a necessary and integral part of their houses and villas, whether in the town or in the country. A common feature of early Roman houses was a small vegetable garden positioned to the rear of the property, enclosed by high walls.

The Roman town houses (*Domus*) were densely packed together in a grid pattern and had a front door opening onto the street. There was a pavement fronting each property, and some of the houses were converted into shops. The design of these houses was mostly uniform in the early times of Roman Italy, and one of the main features was an *atrium tuscanicum*, possibly a development from an Etruscan idea. All the rooms of the house opened into the atrium which was in the centre of the building, and was a rectangular space open to the air with roofs sloping inwards towards it (Diagram A). It also served as a catchment area for collecting water from the roof. Any falling rainwater was directed into a basin or reservoir, known as the *impluvium*, and when water was required it was drawn off from a cistern positioned at the side of the *impluvium*. It is thought that in towns the water supply was not constant and probably in very short supply during long periods of drought in the summer. This method of collecting rainwater was therefore very important in providing clean water for drinking, cooking and for watering plants in the garden.

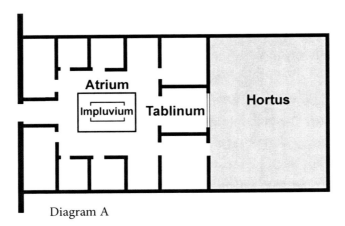

Diagram A

Besides having an atrium, the town house also included a *tablinum* and a *hortus* (garden). The *tablinum* was positioned opposite to the atrium and the entrance door and generally used as the master's bedroom. On entering the house by the door you could have a view through to the *tablinum.* This room was usually entered by an open doorway with a rear window giving a view of the rear garden and the entrance door at the front of the house. The rear garden or *hortus* seems to have been used for growing vegetables.

Archaeological digging at the Roman Villa Regina at Boscoreale, using the most modern methods, discovered a vineyard surrounding the villa. Next to the villa there was evidence of a hortus which seemed to be divided into several vegetable plots by using raised edges to define the different areas, suggesting that a crop rotation system might have been used. Somewhere near the centre of the garden was the remains of a cistern or well which would have provided the water necessary to produce vegetables for culinary use. In the second and first centuries BC the basic town house layout was adapted to include a peristyle garden behind the tablinum as in diagram B. Another variation was to have a peristyle garden in the centre of the house as in diagram C where build-

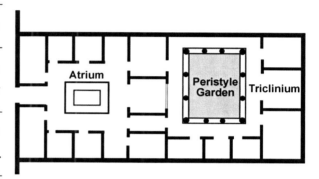

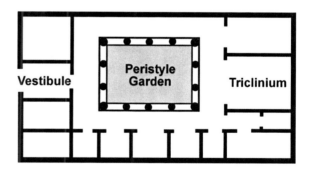

ing space was limited, and where more space was available there would be a hortus to the rear of the property.

Improvements and extensions to the basic town house design probably depended on the wealth of the individual. Houses on a large scale could only be afforded by aristocrats or leading officials. The House of the Faun in Pompeii is such an example and according to the author Maureen Carroll it appeared to have the remains of an orchard and

possibly a vegetable plot to the rear of the house. It is possible that this property was actually a Royal Palace and is regarded as one of the finest examples of Greco-Roman architecture. It has all the features of the houses we have already discussed, but on a much grander scale. Many examples of all the types of house mentioned are in a far more preserved condition in Pompeii than in any other Roman town or city, due to being buried in volcanic ash and lapilli by Vesuvius. The inhabitants of Pompeii appear to have been very fortunate in having reliable water supplies and in the early days of Roman occupation the rainwater was collected in cisterns below the impluvium. This was supplemented by boring at least 100 feet to penetrate water bearing strata below layers of lava from Vesuvius and building well heads. By the second century BC, plentiful supplies of spring water from the nearby mountains of Avelino were canalised at a time when the population of Pompeii was at its peak. At this point in time the Romans were ousted by a Hellenistic invasion. Later, when the Romans returned to Pompeii they supplied piped water to all the inhabitants of the city by utilising the large quantities of spring water available, and with the possible addition of water provided by an aqueduct supplying Naples and Miseno (built *circa* 20 BC). Under the previous Roman occupation of the town piped water was only available to the privileged few. In order to distribute the water under sufficient pressure, several water towers were built incorporating a means of filtration. Public fountains to provide drinking water were positioned at every street corner, consisting of a plain square stone trough with a thick carved slab of stone erected on its side spouting water from a pipe. Many of the houses of aristocratic persons had ornamental fountains and fishponds in their courtyards and gardens.

Pliny the Younger described his Roman villa garden in his Laurentine near Ostia in one of his letters to his friend Gallus: Bordering his drive was a hedge of box and rosemary. The drive had a turning area featuring a circular bed containing a shady vine which was supported and tied to a pergola. The garden was planted with mulberries which seemed to be thriving though other trees were not doing well. The only

evidence of Pliny's Laurentine villa is contained in the letter to Gallus. There are archaeological sites which have been excavated near Ostia but it is not certain any of them fit his description.

The Villa of Poppaea at Oplontis (first century AD) is an exceptional example and must have been impressive in its day for its extensive formal gardens. Excavations revealed gardens within and surrounding the villa with its courtyards and peristyles connecting the various parts of the building. To the rear of the building is a large garden or park, which

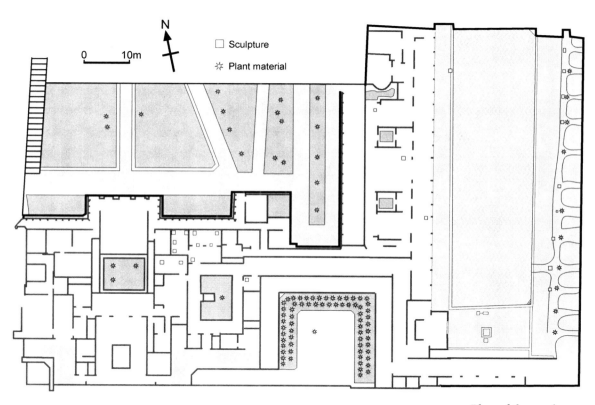

Plan of the gardens at the *villa urbana* of Poppaea at Oplontis.

has been partially excavated to reveal an open area in the middle with central pathways and pathways around the side borders, which have statues. Also, statues were regularly spaced around the sides in borders planted with trees and shrubs. The villa had a very large swimming pool

on the east side, the outer edge of which was planted with oleanders, lemons and mature plane trees in a row. There were thirteen trees altogether, each one having a statue of a hero or god in front of it. The prospect of this particular site must have been awe inspiring, with views of Vesuvius and the sea surrounded by gardens and classical architecture. Certain parts of the garden have been replanted and it now has trimmed hedges of box and oleander following the original design. It is interesting to note that archaeologists can discover where trees and shrubs have grown in the past by impressions left by their root systems and taking casts of the cavities left in the soil. Also, samples of pollen make it possible to identify the species that once grew there.

Another example of a small roman villa garden is at Conimbriga in Portugal. It has a courtyard in which the whole space is taken up by a pool, and is known as the "House of the Jets of Water". It has been renovated and replanted to some extent and consists of six planting boxes constructed of stone and having a geometric shape within the pool. Water is sprayed into the pool by 400 lead jets from within the pool and from the edges of the planting boxes.

In most of the Roman Empire, examples of larger villas, probably built for the nobility and the wealthy rulers, have been discovered. They were known as *villa urbanae* and generally were of three basic designs similar in many ways to those built in Italy. The simplest type, can be described as two rectangular buildings joined together in the middle by a central building sometimes having a pillared entrance, and consisting of a west and an east wing with an entrance in the centre. Courtyard gardens were a feature in the other two types, and in the case of the larger villas there was more than one garden. A second type had buildings on three sides of the courtyard, and in the third the garden would be enclosed on four sides with a peristyle courtyard. It is thought that some villas had borders of decorative plants and possibly box hedges within their courts. There are two sites which had rectangular fishponds, one example at Ectternach in Luxembourg and another at Eccles in Kent. The ponds occupied a large part of the courts, which were open on the south side, and could be viewed from within the peristyle villas.

The Roman palace at Fishbourne in West Sussex is a good example of how the garden was closely linked to the architecture of the building. Extensive excavations carried out in the twentieth century show that it follows the basic design of a Roman villa although it is of substantial proportions. The main courtyard would have been entered by a peri-styled portico and visitors guided along a central path to be received possibly in a reception room in the west wing to the rear of the building complex. Archaeologists found trenches each side of the central path which may have contained box hedges. The east wing, which contained the main entrance hall to the complex, included a northern and southern peristyle 'atrium' or courtyard garden. More recent digs suggest that they contained pools supplied by streams and surrounded by a 'natural garden'. The palace was estimated to have been built *circa* 75 AD for a very important person. It is possible that the owner was Cogidubnus or Togidubnus, a British inhabitant who was probably awarded Roman citizenship during the reign of Emperor Claudius.

The development of the city of Rome owed a lot to the competition between wealthy aristocrats, generals and emperors who wanted to make their mark and influence their citizens into believing that their buildings were the most impressive. Included with the buildings were public and imperial parks, avenues of trees, and gardens. The major construction of Rome really began in the middle of the first century BC, and a plan of the city made of marble, known as the "Marble Plan of Rome" (dated to the early part of the third century AD) shows how it would have looked at the time. Pompey the Great, a very important general who became a wealthy aristocrat, built a complex known as Porticus Pompeiana in the centre of the city in 55 BC. This consisted of a grove or several avenues of trees, a basilica, markets and a theatre with a semi-circular auditorium of impressive size. Adjoining the theatre was a large square with a central pathway leading to the theatre and to either side of this were two colonnades and a grove of trees.

During their campaigns in Asia and the eastern Mediterranean, some of the Roman generals, including Pompey, would have seen the Persian and Hellenistic cities and been impressed by their parks and public buildings. On their return to Rome they paraded items that they had plundered, including sculptures, slaves and even trees. Pliny states that Roman generals returned to Italy from Syria and the eastern Mediterranean with trees including apricots, cherries, peaches and pistachios.

In Pompey's park stood originals and copies from the eastern Greek world.

Emperor Trajan built his own forum in 112 AD; some of it still exists and the outline of it can be seen in the "Marble Plan of Rome". An archaeological dig in 1982 showed that what appeared in the marble plan as dots turned out to be trees planted in four avenues. It had been assumed that the dots represented columns or statues facing the basilica.

Indian Mughal Gardens

India was the last of the countries to be influenced by the spread of the Islamic religion, which first emerged in Persia. The Muslim invasion of India occurred in 1200 AD, although their influence on garden design did not become evident until 1526 when Babur, a Mughal emperor from Turkey, arrived.

The Mughals introduced the *Chahar Bagh* garden to the local Indian culture, but it was not readily accepted due to the unique Hindu approach to art. Eventually, as happened in both Spain and India, the influence of local traditions brought about their own concept of the Islamic garden. Indian gardens bear a loose resemblance to the *Chahar Bagh* design by retaining the geometric shapes typical of this concept.

Three Mughal gardens worthy of study are Chasma Shahi, Anguri Bagh and the Shalimar garden.

The Chasma Shahi (The Royal Spring) is on a fairly steep hillside near Lake Dal in Kashmir and was built by Shah Jahan in 1632. It was irrigated by water that first emerged from a pavilion at the highest point of the garden. The water descended to the lower garden terraces and eventually flowed into a pool at the bottom. This garden was not quartered as in the typical *Chahar Bagh* design, but halved, with the cascades of water channelled down the centre and plants and flowers on either side.

The Anguri Bagh (Garden of the Grapes) near Lake Dal is closer to the *Chahar Bagh* layout and was again built by Shah Jahan. Viewed from above it resembles a quartered garden. At the highest level of the terraced garden is a marble tank which faces the Khas Mahal Palace. Leading from this is a shallow channel which allows water to cascade into a small pool on the lower terrace. A water pipe carries water from the pool on the central axis of the garden to a marble water tank in the centre where pathways intersect. The flower beds are divided into four by the footpaths instead of water channels, following the *chahar*

bagh design. In the past the four beds contained attractive flowering plants and low growing shrubs. The garden has in the recent past been neglected and though the structure of the channels, pool and pathways still exist, water is absent.

The Shalimar Garden (Abode of Bliss) is situated near Lahor in Pakistan and is one of the largest gardens built by the Emperor Shah Jahan. It was finished around 1643 AD. The design is based on two *Chahar Baghs*, one on each side of a central waterway fed by a canal, which is in turn connected to the Ravi River. The canal provided the water for a large tank, containing at least one hundred fountains, at the highest level of terracing. The garden is constructed on a slope and there are three levels of terracing. The lowest terrace was intended for visitors. The top terrace was the most private, and had a pavilion at the centre overlooking the central waterway where the Emperor could view the entire garden from the highest point.

The Shalimar garden is surrounded by high walls, which would have excluded the public originally. However, it is now open to anyone who wishes to admire and enjoy this spectacular garden of fountains. The four corners feature small octagonal towers built onto red sandstone pavilions and the garden is today entered by the top terrace, allowing an impressive view of the water channels and fountains.

The large pool in the centre of the garden is part of the middle terrace and features a hundred fountains that look like lotus buds emerging from the surface and spraying water in a regular pattern around the pool. The pool is square, each side measuring approximately 100 metres. In the middle is a small patio edged with ornately carved white marble balustrading, where the emperor could enjoy the cooling water and contemplate the scene. Two red sandstone pavilions flank the pool to the left and the right.

The retaining wall which supports the central terrace was originally adapted so that it could contain several flower vases within it. The wall also provided a means of supporting lanterns on a shelf allowing illumination of the garden at night. There are parallel paths either side of the water channels and the rest of the quartered areas are grassed. Looking along the central axis of the garden the view of the water channels is uninterrupted, but to the left and right is a row of mature mango trees whose spreading branches provide cool shade.

This Mughal garden was evidently designed for pleasure like several others, but some gardens contained mausoleums. These mausoleums did not follow the Persian tradition, but possibly had a Mongolian or Hindu influence. It was quite common for the gardens to be created and established while the Mughal was still living. His tomb would be built in the centre of the garden ready for the entombing of his body when he died, which is similar to the tradition of the Pharaohs of ancient Egypt. When the Mughal died, the mausoleum garden would be opened to the public.

However, the most famous *Chahar Bagh* is possibly the simplest and most perfectly formed — it is the tomb complex of Mumtaz Mahal at Agra, usually known as the Taj Mahal. The Taj Mahal is a mausoleum created by Emperor Shah Jahan in the seventeenth century in memory of his favourite wife, Mumtaz Mahal, who died in childbirth. The garden is based on the traditional *Chahar Bagh* design except that the mausoleum is at the end of the water channel, which is filled with a row of fountains. The vista from the elaborate entrance gateway to the white marble tomb is dramatic, and is emphasised by a line of narrowly columnar cypresses either side of the canal and its surrounding paths.

Islamic Gardens in Spain

Muslims, commonly known as Moors, who came from North African stock that had converted to Islam, invaded the Iberian Peninsula early in the eighth century. Muslim occupation was not officially recognised until later in the eighth century when the few remaining members of the Ummayad Dynasty from Damascus fled to Andalusia when they were overthrown by the Abbasid Dynasty. One of the survivors, Abd-ar-Rahman I, became the first crowned ruler or Emir at Cordova. When the Moors invaded Spain, evidence of Roman occupation was still present and may have influenced their thinking as regards architecture, gardens, and irrigation systems.

Compared with the culture in Europe at the time, the Moors were very advanced and established Universities studying mathematics, science and medicines. They were highly skilled in art and design and were able to produce items wrought from various metals, such as iron, bronze, gold and silver, and exported pottery and textiles.

There is little evidence remaining of the many gardens that were said to be in existence by the tenth century in the country areas surrounding Cordova. Like the Romans they produced irrigation systems to provide water for their houses, baths, orchards, vineyards and gardens. Aqueducts were built to carry the water from the hillsides and rivers to where it was required, and it has been suggested that the demand must have been great as laws were introduced to control its use.

The best example of Islamic gardens still existing from the fourteenth century is the Alhambra. Its name is derived from the Arabic name Qal'at al'Hamra and is sometimes known as the "red fort" as it is built from the red stone of the area. Its fortified buildings are built on a hill known as Sabikah and they overlook the city of Grenada below.

The Alhambra is a complex of many buildings and is based on the fortress which is thought to have been in existence since the ninth century. It became established as a royal residence in the thirteenth century

when the Nasrite dynasty was founded by Muhammed Al-Ahmar. Before construction of the residence could begin, the fortress required restoration. This commenced in 1238 and the building work was continued by his son Muhammed II and his successors. The building of the royal palaces took place during the reigns of Yusuf I (1333–54) and Muhammed V (1354–92). In 1492 the Islamic reign ended when Grenada was conquered by the Catholic Monarchs (Ferdinand and Isabella). Further additions were made to the Alhambra in later centuries, such as a church and a Franciscan monastery by Charles V (1516–56) and Philip V (1700–46).

There is something special and unique about the Alhambra in that it is like a series of rooms with high walls, some indoors and some outdoors, featuring ornate halls, pools, and trickling water in rills and fountains. There are arcades and porticos which conform to a traditional Arabic style decorated with lattice fretwork and many with inscriptions of Arabic script formed into intricate patterns. Views into the courtyards or patios allow panoramas of the hills and mountains beyond. Several patios are a feature here, and the idea is an adaptation of the Roman atrium in which a central pool was integral, with the later addition of the fountain in the centre. Islamic garden designers incorporated this idea and put their own interpretation upon it. The Arabian people's desire for water influenced their need for it to be a feature in their "Gardens of Paradise". The pools in the centres of the courtyards are connected by irrigation channels and are mainly rectangular or circular in shape. Unlike the Roman pools they are just below the floor level and surrounded by mosaic tiles or stone paving. The "Court of the Myrtles" is notable for its Islamic architecture; its pool is rectangular with a water spout at each end facing the south and north porticos. There are two hedges of myrtle parallel with the pool, and the pool reflects an image of the Tower of Comares, the official residence of the caliph, and the porticos, like a mirror. One of the most attractive features is the Court of the Lions which has a central fountain consisting of a twelve-sided basin supported by twelve marble

lions spouting water. The water falls into a shallow trough and runs into four narrow channels which divide the court into four parts. This animal sculpture is not typical of Islamic art and its design is thought to be influenced by the Jewish vizier Yusuf b. Naghrallah (eleventh century). The four parts are planted with foliage and flowering plants, a few clipped bushes in gravel, or just gravel. The variation in planting is probably due to the need to replace the plants and shrubs occasionally to retain a tidy appearance. Around the four sides of the patio are a series of 124 columns which are exquisite, being decorative as well as functional, and which support arcades and two porticos. These columns have been likened to a grove of palm trees and the fountain as an oasis.

The *Generalife* is a part of the Alhambra citadel that was built for Yusef I and Mohammed V as their summer residence, and dates from the thirteenth century. It is separated from the main buildings of the Alhambra by a small valley and is situated at a higher level. Its name is derived from Jinan al-Arif which can be translated to 'gardens of the overseer'. It is famous for its summer gardens and can be entered by going through the house leading to the Patio de la Acequia (The Court of the Long Pond) which features a long central canal. The courtyard is rectangular with a path halfway along which crosses in the centre of the water course and includes a small circular pond spouting water from a lotus bud fountain. The central path quarters the garden, creating the traditional *Chahar Bagh*, although it is built fifty centimetres above the original one, due to the build up of debris and earth over five centuries. The archaeologist Jesus Bermudez excavated the site in 1959 and revealed the original pavement. The garden was re-planted following the excavation and since its inception it has been altered several times.

In the four quartered flower beds are hedges of trimmed myrtle, roses, cypress and orange trees — it is a luxuriant paradise in its own right. At the north and south end of the courtyard are porticos with shallow circular water basins set into the paving, spouting water from a lotus-bud fountain. Along the length of the central canal, jets of water arch over it and splash into it. This is a much later addition and does not conform to the original design.

The fountain at the Patio de la Acequia in the Alhambra Citadel.

Medieval Gardens

After the Romans left Britain, their gardens were abandoned and fell into disuse. Nothing of any importance occurred until the monasteries were gradually introduced to Britain. When these monastic communities became established, the monks used their skills to establish farms, and particularly gardens. They were self-sufficient, well able to produce all their needs for food and medicines. The monks were well educated, and evidence for this can be found in the records they kept of day to day life, including the design and management of their gardens.

In general their gardens were divided into separate parts according to their needs. For instance, there were kitchen gardens for the growing of vegetables, herbs and fruit for culinary purposes, and it is reasonable to assume that the larger monasteries had orchards for fruit trees. Many of the monastic establishments had what could be called ornamental gardens, possibly for quiet contemplation rather than for pleasure. Besides having orchards, some of the larger monasteries had vineyards which were capable of producing wines for their own use and probably for other secular establishments not having the ideal conditions. Many of the fruit trees and plants were introductions from European monasteries, typical examples being grape vines, medlar, mulberry, pears, plums, quince and rosemary. Native fruit trees were also grown but to begin with they may have experimented to find the best ones for cropping and suitability; vigour, for instance, could be controlled by grafting onto suitable rootstocks. The Bishop of Winchester in the thirteenth century employed a gardener to carry out grafting of fruit trees and paid him one shilling. Plans of early monastic gardens showed that the fruit trees were mainly planted in rows and spaced to allow sufficient growth, light and air. Apart from the orchard, the gardens tended to be formal with beds arranged in a geometric pattern; they were mainly rectangular and bordered by paths. The beds were quite narrow, allowing for cultivation of plants without treading on the soil.

Herbs grown for medicinal purposes were usually grown in beds near to the infirmary for easy access. Flowers were also considered necessary for decorating the church. Scented herbs and flowers were strewn on the floors to disguise bad smells, and it was also believed that this would give protection from pests and diseases to the monks and people. Some of the monastic gardens were open to the community, although some monasteries had enclosed gardens or precincts which were designated for the Abbot. "At Abingdon the kitchener, precentor sacrist and keeper of works all had their own gardens". (James Bond, *Monastic Landscapes*, *p*.154)

Excavations at Mount Grace Priory in Yorkshire have added to our knowledge of the practices of the hermit-like order of Carthusian Monks who lived there in the 14th century, revealing that each monk had his own garden attached to his living quarters or cell.

Anne Jennings, *Medieval Gardens*, p.20

The origin of monasticism goes back to St Anthony who was born in Egypt circa 250 AD, lived in the Egyptian desert and was the first Coptic monk; later he had many devoted followers who asked for his religious instruction. As a Christian convert he spent some time living as a hermit in the desert where, with some irrigation, he was able to subsist on what he grew in his garden. The establishment of Coptic Monasteries spread throughout Egypt, and after a hundred years they were also to be found in Syria and Palestine. One of St Anthony's devotees, Pachomius (290–346), was responsible for establishing several monasteries in Egypt.

Pachomius laid down rules that monks should spend some time in isolation in order to learn from solitary contemplation, but that it was important to experience a communal life. In *Monastic Landscapes*, James Bond writes: "Several of the earliest monastic codes, including the Rule of St Benedict, required gardens to be enclosed within the precinct for the solace and sustenance of the monks." (*p*.153). There was a

necessity, therefore, to enclose most of the gardens in order to keep the general public out. The enclosures were in some cases constructed of stone, but also hedges formed from trimmed hawthorn and blackthorn made a good prickly barrier capable of keeping people and wild animals out. Another alternative was wicker or interwoven fencing made from the flexible stems of coppiced hazel and willow. In the countryside the peasants had their own plots of land where they could grow vegetables and herbs, and they constructed their own woven fencing mainly to keep livestock and wild animals out.

Many of the plants grown in the early monastery gardens came from Europe, but a substantial amount of horticultural knowledge was gained from the classical world of Greece and Rome. It is worth noting that the Greeks and Romans occupied Egypt, and it is reasonable to suppose that they would have learned something from the Egyptian gardens and their designs). A herbal text book by Apuleius Platonicus, apparently produced around 400 AD, became available about 1000 AD translated into Old English. It is known that the knowledgeable or 'Venerable Bede' referred to Pliny the Elder's encyclopaedia for information on the growing of herbs for medicinal and culinary use. The Abbey of Bury St Edmunds compiled a beautifully illustrated herbal text, which combined information from Apuleius and Pliny, early in the twelfth century.

It is not known whether the cultivation of vines continued after the end of the Roman occupation of Britain. However, Bede maintained that in the eighth century the production of wine from grapes was commonplace in southern parts of England. King Alfred considered that monastic vineyards were sufficiently important to need a law which allowed compensation if they were damaged.

The Romans were responsible for introducing apple varieties that were sweet enough to be eaten as a dessert, unlike our indigenous crab-apples. Again it is not known whether the early monastic establishments re-introduced these varieties or whether they were survivors from Roman times.

THE BEGINNINGS OF THE FORMAL GARDEN

A notable monastery in Switzerland, St Gallen, established in the early ninth century, produced a plan for their gardens which still survives today. In this plan the cemetery garden featured a planting scheme that included apples, pears, cherries, plums, peaches, fig, mulberry, quince, medlar and service. The kitchen garden featured vegetables and potherbs which were as follows: beet, parsnips, radishes, lettuce, celery, chervil, coriander, dill, black cumin, parsley, savory, poppy, garlic, leeks, onions and shallots.

Some of the monasteries had large estates which were not necessarily attached to the monastery and managed by an Abbot or Prior. Abbots often had manor houses with walled gardens next to them, like Abbot William Colerne of Malmesbury in the later part of the thirteenth century. His Purton Manor had two pools constructed in the garden and another one at Crudwell. These manor gardens were usually formal, often having a square lawn in the centre, sometimes divided by paths, and with borders for flowering plants or herbs surrounding it. Meadow turf was normally laid on carefully levelled ground and when established the grass was kept short by skilful scything.

The green turf which is in the middle of the material cloister refreshes encloistered eyes and their [the monks] desire to study returns. It is truly the nature of the colour green that it nourishes the eye and preserves the vision.

Hugh of Fouilloy (*c.*1132–1152)

Manor houses were not just the preserve of the monasteries. The landed gentry or the lords and ladies of the court and the monarchy in medieval times also lived in manor houses. Their gardens were similar in design to the monastic gardens, but some would have been more elaborate with ornate fencing and pergolas dividing the garden. Some featured pools and fountains supplied by diverting a stream or spring. Rills or channels arranged in a formal pattern fed water by gravity to create fountains. It is thought that the more elaborate European gardens created in the medieval period may have been influenced by Persian and Roman designs for fountains and gardens.

In England, parks were created solely to provide places in the country where the kings and noblemen could occasionally enjoy sport and relaxation in safety away from the people and the worries of state. These parks were enclosed by brick or stone walls, and areas for riding and hunting were created by thinning out or felling some of the natural forest if necessary. Sometimes, trees and shrubs were planted to give sufficient cover for rabbits, hares and deer.

3

PLANTS AND FLOWERS
PORTRAYED IN ART

Flowers were frequently used by the Ancient Egyptians for special occasions such as festivals, funerals and to decorate the tombs of pharaohs and gods. Depending on the occasion, the flowers were combined into bouquets, garlands and collars. In the present day, Egyptians celebrate religious festivals by parading the streets playing musical instruments, and carrying flowers and palm leaves. Such moments in time were illustrated on some ancient Egyptian tombs, where people, though mainly officials or priests, were shown carrying papyrus and lotus flowers in procession. The papyrus and lotus flowers seemed to be used most frequently either separately or in bunches or combined in a bouquet with other flowers. The lotus flower in particular was highly prized for having sacred and symbolical qualities, and the Blue Lotus was notable for its scent. Papyrus was used to represent the resurrection of the deceased.

A typical formal stick bouquet was formed using a strong base material, such as the stems of reeds (*Phragmitis australis*) or papyrus cut off close to the base to provide sufficient length. Some of the stick bouquets could be at least the height of a man, maybe 2 metres or more in

length. The stems were bound together to create a firm base to which were added various flowers which had as much length of stem as possible. A binding twine was used to tie the flowers into the base and they were arranged in tiers along the length of the bouquet with sufficient space between each tier to allow the bouquet to be held for carrying. Depending upon the time of year, the flowers of the blue and the white lotus were used, combined with blue cornflower and red poppy with the addition of mandrake fruits. On some occasions fresh flowers were not used, perhaps because they would not last long enough or it was the time of year when few flowers were available. This could explain why at other times some tombs contained garlands and collars which had faience beads attached in regular patterns, made to represent fruits, leaves and petals.

Floral decorations were found on Tutankhamun's coffin, and according to Percy Newberry they were in a remarkable state of preservation. The flowers could easily be identified even though King Tutankhamun was buried in 1339 BC, but they were so delicate that some of them disintegrated when touched. The innermost coffin featured the famous golden face of Tutankhamun and around it was the most beautiful floral tribute in the form of a collar. One has to imagine the colours of the flowers, fruits and leaves when they were fresh to appreciate what it must have looked like. The collar was based on papyrus pith, and sewn on to it were blue faience beads, flowers and fruit arranged in nine rows. It was composed of blue lotus petals, yellow flowers of oxtongue, blue cornflower, red berries of woody or withania nightshade, halved yellow mandrake fruits, leaves of olive, willow, pomegranate and strips of date palm leaves to which were attached the berries of woody nightshade.

The artists who painted pictures of the plants growing in Egypt were highly skilled and their work represented plants in a stylised way, but almost every species is instantly recognisable. Sometimes their botanical designs might only feature a part of the plant, for instance the flowers only in a piece of jewellery or in a tomb painting. The white and

blue lotus water lilies and the papyrus were the most commonly used because of their symbolical importance (the lotus represented Upper Egypt and the papyrus the kingdom of Lower Egypt — the two combined represented the unified country of Egypt).

Plants were engraved or carved in relief in tomb paintings and on columns inside and outside tombs, temples and other important buildings. Some columns were carved to represent the bundled stems of papyrus with the capitals featuring the stylised form of the flowers. The lotus flower also featured in stylised form on the capitals of stone columns. Before stone was used to construct buildings, temporary structures were built using bundles of papyrus bound together to support a light roof.

Among the many treasures found in King Tutankhamun's tomb

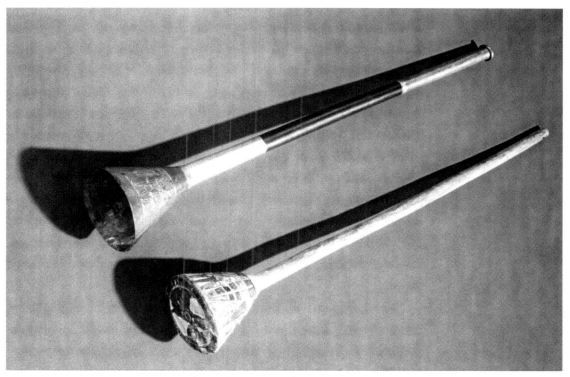

Trumpet and wooden stopper, from the Tomb of Tutankhamun (c.1370-1352 BC) New Kingdom (bronze or copper with gold overlay) by Egyptian 18th Dynasty (c.1567–1320 BC). Egyptian National Museum, Cairo.

63

were two trumpets, one of silver and the other of copper. They are long and elegantly shaped, like Victorian coaching post horns, with flared bell-ends. The slender stems represented lotus stalks, and the flared ends the flowers, with engravings of the sepals and petals on the outside of the silver trumpet. In addition, the trumpets had closely fitting wooden cores, with the solid bell portion decorated and coloured like a water lily. The silver trumpet was actually played in 1939 by a military bandsman in the Egyptian Museum in Cairo and was recorded for BBC radio. It produced a sound that was softer and more melodious than the post horn, though the range of notes was the same.

A few temples, mainly those discovered in Amarna, featured representations of the palm tree in stone columnar form, though the remains of the pillars and capitals are fragmentary. According to W. Stevenson Smith, the well known archaeologist William Flinders Petrie (1853–1942) found fragments of a capital which featured realistically carved bunches of dates, and palm fronds were carved on another fragment and seemingly anticipated the Roman columns at Philae. The capitals of the columns at the late Eygptian-Roman site of Philae were quite ornate with carved palm fronds at the top which were reflexed near the leaf tips, with the leaf stalk or mid-ribs equally spaced around the circumference giving a more linear shape to the pinnate leaf (in reality the leaf-frond is broader). Attached to each alternate leaf stalk in two-dimensional form was a bunch of dates on either side. Just below the bunches of dates where the leaf stalk effectively joins the trunk of the palm tree the column was carved in such a way to show the typical base markings of the fronds when they are chopped off close to the trunk.

Representations of plants feature on many artefacts belonging to the Pharaohs, including furniture, jewellery, vases and bowls. Some of the items were used for ritualistic purposes while others were for comfort and pleasure. The discovery of King Tutankhamun's tomb revealed several well-preserved pieces of furniture including a decorative chest possibly used for the storage of clothes. It is wooden, with panels of

ivory and ebony, and one of the end panels shows the King hunting in
the marshes with a bow and arrow; his Queen sits in the foreground

End panel of
Wooden Casket
from King
Tutankhamun's
Tomb.

holding an arrow. The long side panels feature a pool in the centre containing fish, surrounded by motifs of red poppies, blue cornflowers and
the fruits of the mandrake. The lid depicts the King sitting in a garden
and being presented with flowers by the Queen. The Golden Throne is
very special; its main feature on the back is King Tutankhamun and
Queen Ankhesenamun wearing floral collars. To the right of them is a
small table or wooden frame with floral garlands decorating the stays
of the legs and what appears to be a wreath on the table top. Three vertical struts support the back of the chair, and between these is featured
a papyrus thicket with birds flying out of it.

The Eighteenth Dynasty in Egypt was notable for its fine craftsmanship in furniture, jewellery, and for producing delightful small objects regarded as luxuries rather than perhaps for functional use. One such item is a coloured ivory ointment spoon, now in the Brooklyn Museum,

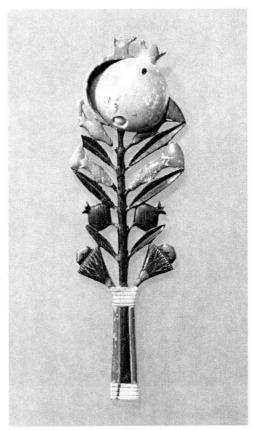

Ointment spoon (painted ivory). Brooklyn Museum of Art.

which was fashioned to resemble a pomegranate spray or small branch. It consists of a handle at the base, and the stem has leaves and flowers attached and two tiny fruits of the pomegranate. The top of the stem or handle is hollowed out to be used as a spoon but in outline it is in the distinctive shape of the pomegranate fruit.

Examples of flower motifs in jewellery include the pair of gold earrings found in Sety II's (1200–1194 BC) tomb (known as the Gold Tomb in the Valley of the Kings). Each earring consists of a concave front stud made from a fine gold foil to represent an eight petalled flower of an unidentified type. The rear stud is linked to the front stud by an interlocking tube or bar and a trapezoidal pendant is attached which on both sides bears Sety's cartouches. Suspended from this are seven cornflower pendants connected by tubular stalks, arranged in two rows, with three larger flowers in the lower row. The spherical part of the flower is formed from two ribbed hollow halves to which has been added a flared rim.

Gold earrings found in Sety II's tomb.

In tomb paintings, banqueting scenes frequently feature guests wearing floral collars, and many imitations of these using stones or faience beads have been found in tombs. One particular example can be found in the Metropolitan Museum, New York, and it comes from the Eighteenth Dynasty (1350 BC). The terminals are inlaid to represent the white lotus flower and includes the white petals of the lotus flower in a blocked pattern. Attached to the blade shaped terminals are five rows of pendants spaced between faience beads of white, dark brown, green, yellow, the inner most one with yellow, blue, brown and green beads. The first row represents the white petals of the lotus flower; the second represents fruits of the date; the third green date palm leaves; the fourth fruits of the mandrake. The innermost ones appear to imitate fruits of the pomegranate, brown and green seed pods of the poppy, and the blue ones the cornflower.

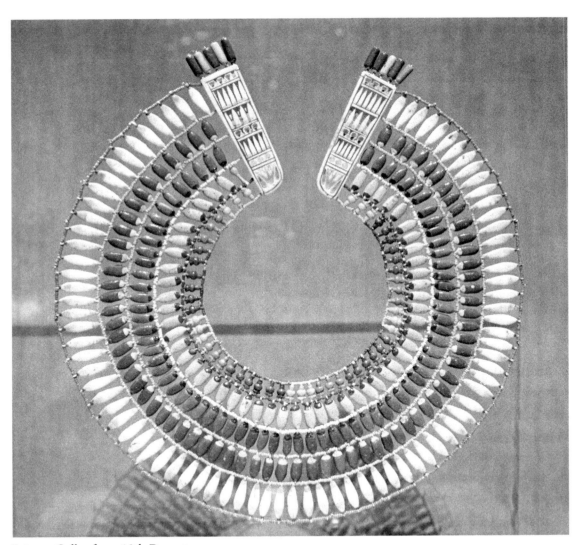

Faience Collar from 18th Dynasty.

4

GARDENERS IN PHARAONIC TIMES

In ancient Egypt the description "gardener" could be applied to a simple labourer being supervised by a foreman, or to an important official employed by the Pharaoh to design gardens. Some gardeners of high rank had the responsibility of providing vegetables, plants and flowers as daily offerings to the Gods or a deceased Pharaoh. It was believed that a dead Pharaoh lived in the heavens by day and returned at night to his tomb where the food offerings would replenish him. Offerings were also provided for feasts at the beginning of each season where the kings, princes and important officials would partake of the remaining food. Other ceremonies such as the opening of the dykes by the Pharaoh during the inundation and the representation of the marriage of the God Horus to Hathor the cow goddess were very important. The vast quantities of produce required for these events was very demanding for the official and the many garden labourers that would have to be employed.

The task of creating gardens and the basic landscape was sometimes left to official architects who were answerable only to the Pharaoh. One such person was Senenmut, the architect involved with the design of the gardens integral with the mortuary temple built for Hatshepsut, the female Pharaoh and wife of Tuthmosis II.

The gardeners and agricultural labourers had a very hard life according to ancient Egyptian texts, and were expected to work from dawn to dusk. Many of the tombs contained small figures modelled in wood or fired clay pottery (known as *Shabtis*) about 2 to 3 inches long, representing workers. According to Alix Wilkinson in her book *The Garden in Ancient Egypt* (p.28) they were often inscribed with commands that they must water the crops and cultivate the fields. It was believed that these figures would continue the regular toil in the afterlife for the Pharaoh and their most important officials.

The gardeners' tasks were many and varied and in such a dry climate regular watering was necessary to keep the crops growing. After the inundation of the lands the fields and gardens suitable for crops needed to be prepared before sowing and planting could take place. Agricultural labourers and possibly gardeners were required to move soil or silt to level the ground, and to create temporary mud dams to hold surplus water and create irrigation channels. The tools used were primitive; soil was carried in baskets, and digging was achieved by the use of a type of hoe where the blade is drawn towards you. A later development in Egypt was the plough pulled by oxen and guided by a labourer behind the plough, which was more efficient.

The close proximity of the desert to the fertile areas surrounding the Nile meant that strong winds blew sand onto the soil, which had to be removed to prevent the smothering of plants. As if this was not enough to frustrate the gardener, he also had to contend with birds and monkeys attacking fruit trees and vines for their fruit. The foliage of vegetables, trees and summer wheat could be eaten by goats, geese, locusts and even the hippopotami that lived in the Nile during the Pharaonic period. The gardener did what he could to defend his crops, building high walls for protection where they could be afforded.

Information about the names of the gardeners is quite scarce, particularly before the Hellenistic period. One individual by the name of Nakht had a tomb in Thebes and was described as being 'gardener of the divine offerings of Amun'. He supervised the growing and supply

of a huge amount of flowers which were put together to produce bouquets for offering tables during the reign of Amenophis III (*c*.1375 BC). Important officials who served the Pharaohs had their own tomb chapels and gardens and employed gardeners to maintain and supply offerings after their demise.

Historians have differing opinions about whether the cultivated land was under Pharaonic ownership entirely. In some instances it has been said that wealthy individuals and even peasantry were granted the freehold of land for services to the King. Just like Roman soldiers who committed great acts of bravery and were outstanding in battle, Egyptian soldiers were given land when they retired. It is likely, however, that Alexander did take full possession of the land irrespective of what happened before, and that when he died Ptolemy inherited all the land of Egypt and became the first member of the dynasty. It is thought that the Ptolemy dynasty was responsible for draining the Fayum marshes, and converting the region into a highly productive area for fruits, vegetables and wine. Greek trained gardeners and vintners were brought in to transform the Fayum.

At this time all the agricultural land was divided into estates and given to important officials for them to run. One such official was Apollonios, the Chief financial adviser to the King. They were allowed to make a profit from their produce, although they had to pay taxes which amounted to one-sixth of the annual harvest of wine and fruit from orchards, payable in silver. The equipment required by the employees was provided by the estate owner and they were paid a salary, sometimes given produce for their own consumption, and depending upon their status they may have received a share in the profits.

Among the two thousand papyri written by Zenon is a document that describes the correspondence that took place between Apollonios and his estate officials. Gardeners on the estates were responsible for maintaining plants and trees to produce crops of fruit, vegetables and wine. Sometimes young plants transported from the Memphis region were needed for the estates in the Fayum region. Before this period in

Egyptian history very little is known about the payment of agricultural workers or how owners or tenants were paid by the Pharaoh for wine and fruit grown in the orchards.

5

PLANTS FOR ALL PURPOSES

Native and Imported Plants

During the Pharaonic period of ancient Egypt several plants, shrubs, and trees were introduced and grown with the native species. They probably came from other Middle Eastern countries, and parts of Asia and North Africa. The Egyptian climate was very harsh — it was only the Nile and the irrigation it could provide that made it possible to grow sub-tropical plants.

The Egyptians must have experienced some failures in their efforts to introduce new species, which would have been obtained by collecting seeds or young plants, or even transporting semi-mature trees. A reason for introducing new plant species may have been to provide a wider range of vegetables, fruit and cereals in order to improve their diet. For example, they improved the quality and yield of cereal by introducing a better wheat species than the native Emmer wheat. Egypt along with Britain became known as "The bread basket of the Roman Empire". Another reason may be that the Egyptians wanted to be self sufficient in medicinal herbs.

It is known that Queen Hatshepsut mounted an expedition to the

land of Punt (probably present day Somalia) in the fifteenth century BC (circa 1490 BC) to obtain living incense trees for planting at her mortuary temple at Deir el Bahari west of Thebes. Queen Hatshepsut was the wife of Thutmose II, and later she acted as a Regent for Thutmose III while he became old enough to become Pharaoh. In fact, she seems to have ruled Egypt as a Pharaoh until she died, while her nephew fought wars for his country until she died.

Her actual role is subject to speculation but she must have been a remarkable woman; however, all that is left of her are a few defaced statues and her magnificent mortuary temple. Her project to obtain incense trees was very ambitious and ground breaking, especially when one considers that the attempt to transplant semi-mature trees had probably not been tried before. The techniques involved in successfully transplanting trees of substantial size was not perfected in the west until the twentieth century.

The walls of Hatshepsut's mortuary temple, carved in relief, depict the expedition in amazing detail, showing the ships setting out to sail north along the Nile, and then via a canal to the Red Sea. They sailed the entire length of the Red Sea to reach the land of Punt, the whole journey was a distance of approximately two thousand miles, which would have taken several weeks. Having arrived at their destination officials and their labourers went about the task of purchasing thirty-one incense trees. The wall carvings suggest that the roots of the trees were neatly contained, possibly in reed baskets. It is debatable how they managed to keep the root balls moist during the journey back to Egypt. It would have been necessary to water them occasionally; perhaps the baskets were lined with moist clay and they took on board fresh water for this purpose. Before leaving, the ships were laden with "all goodly fragrant – woods of God's land, heaps of myrrh resins, of myrrh-trees, with ebony and pure ivory, with green gold of Emu, with incense. Never was the like of this brought for any King who has been since the beginning." (A translation of the hieroglyphic script on the temple walls from Breasted, *Historic Egypt*, p.276).

Before the reign of Queen Hatshepsut, many of the kings organised trips to this area to obtain Frankincense and Myrrh resin and other valuable items. Experts have debated whether the incense trees were Frankincense (*Boswellia sacra*) or Myrrh (*Commiphora myrrha*), as it is difficult to tell for certain from the images on the temple walls. Both of these resins were valued as highly as gold, and as all Christians know the three kings presented these valuable treasures to Christ in the manger. The resins are obtained by making deep cuts in the bark of the trees. A sticky sap seeps out — Frankincense is milky white and Myrrh is reddish in colour. This is collected and allowed to dry, forming a crystalline substance which is graded for quality before being traded or sold. Frankincense when burned creates a smoke which has a warm fragrance, and in Egypt it was used during ritual worship and for embalming. Myrrh was probably valued for its medicinal properties and as an ingredient in perfume and cosmetics. Both trees can be found growing in desert-like conditions today in Somalia.

The expedition to Punt returned successfully, the boats heavily laden with all their valuable cargo, no doubt to great acclaim. The trees were obtained at great cost and planted on the terraces of the queen's temple at Deir el-Bahri, but it is uncertain whether they survived.

Acacia nilotica

Nile Acacia
Family: Leguminosae

This tree varies in height from 2.5 to 14 metres, depending upon situation and water supply to the roots. It is native to Egypt and naturally occurring in the Nile Valley, Delta region and oases. Today it is widespread throughout Africa, Asia, India and Arabia, mainly in drier areas. However, in Egypt today the tree is becoming scarce and is usually only found growing alongside canals and close to the Nile in the Delta areas, possibly due to the climate being drier than it used to be. The plantations that existed in the Pharaonic period have been cut down in preference for date palm groves.

This Acacia is a very adaptable species. Requirements for rainfall can vary from a few inches to over three feet; where it is low the plant is more like a large shrub in height and is deciduous in the dry season. It prefers drier areas which for most of the year go without rain, and during the hottest parts of the year it drops all of its leaves and becomes dormant. In the Nile Valley and the Delta the Acacia was mainly dependent upon irrigation from the Nile and the canals. The trees growing close to or on the banks of the Nile and canals were much larger, and having a more constant supply of water they tended to remain almost evergreen. The Acacia grows well in alkaline soils, particularly black and alluvial soils, but will withstand saline soils. It is capable of resisting temperatures as high as 50 °C and down to -1 °C, though young tender growths can suffer frost damage. Altitude does not seem to affect it much either, as it is able to grow well typically in the highlands of Sudan or at sea level in the Delta.

Although *Acacia nilotica* is a variable species it has several identifiable features — the bark is thin, fissured, quite rough, dark reddish brown, and the branches are brownish purple. It has several grey sharp spines in pairs which can be about 3 cm long in the leaf axils, hence the

reason for it being called the 'Prickly Acacia'. The leaves are bipinnate, with 3 to 6 pairs of pinnae, each one having numerous leaflets, possibly up to 30, greyish-green with fine hairs. Flowers appear with golden yellow globular heads about 1.5 cm in diameter either in leaf axils or in whorls at the end of the branches. Later, pods develop which can vary in length from 8 to 18 cm, and up to about 2.5 cm in width. The pods are very constricted, almost flat in profile, bulging where the seeds are located, and straight or curved, with very fine grey hairs. Each pod may contain up to sixteen almost black compressed seeds which are ripe in spring or early summer.

Once the pods have turned black they are ready for harvesting and are picked from the trees rather than left to fall to the ground. The seeds are separated by pounding, though it is possible to achieve separation by immersing in water; as they have a very hard seed coat absorption will not occur. In nature, animals have a part to play in the spread of the seeds, which having passed through the digestive system will readily germinate, given sufficient moisture in the soil. To achieve germination of seeds by more conventional means it is necessary to pour boiling water over the seeds, which are left in the water for up to twelve hours. Another method is to chip a part of the seed coat by mechanical means called scarification so that the seed can absorb moisture from the soil in order to germinate. The Egyptians in Pharaonic times may have used this method but it is not ideal for large quantities. These days soaking in acids diluted with water is more convenient though it requires a certain amount of expertise in knowing the correct dilution rate of the acid and how long to soak the seed.

In the past and in ancient Egypt the species was planted in great numbers as an agricultural crop to produce wood handles for hoes and ploughs, and lumber for boats, small boxes and furniture. The timber is twice as hard as teak, resistant to termites, and can be water seasoned to make it waterproof.

When inundation or heavy rains come the trees are stimulated into growth causing the fast rising of sap. The flow is sometimes so excessive

that it exudes gum through cracks in the thin bark. It is probably the means by which the Acacia is able to survive a temporary excess of water which may cause water-logging. The gum exudes naturally from the trunk of the tree forming either round or oval droplets up to about 3.5 cm in diameter, though the gum is exuded more effectively by making incisions in the bark. With exposure to the air the gum hardens and in the case of *Acacia nilotica* is usually white, sometimes slightly yellow. There are other Acacia species that produce gum which is mainly red, but it is considered inferior. When the gum begins to fall to the ground it is ready to collect in baskets or leather sacks and in ancient times was transported by bullocks or camels. Along with other Acacia gums it was taken to well established centres such as Alexandria and Dafur for sale and export. This trade in gum continues to the present day as the Acacia gum is still recognised as an important substance for medicinal use.

When Acacia gum is purchased for use in medicine it is often broken down into small fragments which are usually sharp and angular like glass and almost transparent. Early in the twentieth century it was recommended by British Pharmacopoeia and United States Pharmacopoeia to be given to patients in the form of mucilage composed of small fragments of gum dissolved in water (8 parts gum to 35 parts water) and filtered. A viscous liquid is produced which coats the inflamed surfaces of the digestive respiratory or urinary tract and has a soothing effect. It was considered to be beneficial for treating diarrhoea and dysentery, and also used as an ingredient in cough linctuses. The mucilage mentioned above was sweetened and administered to patients suffering from the early stages of Typhoid fever.

Various parts of the tree were used by African native tribes to treat a wide range of health conditions. The leaves and seed pods are suitable for use as fodder for small livestock and cattle. The pods can be given to the animals whilst still green as a nutritious feed but they prefer dried pods taken directly from Acacia trees or fed to them as a supplement.

The Moors considered that Acacia gum was so nutritious at the time of harvesting that they could virtually depend upon it as their only food source.

Allium cepa

Onion
Family: Liliaceae

The onion has been cultivated since before pre-dynastic times in Egypt when Neolithic people started to settle and till the land to produce food. The plant is very adaptable and widespread throughout the world, and many varieties are available adapted to different climates. Originally it may have come from Persia (Iran). Produced by sowing seed in prepared ground outdoors in the winter preferably near the Nile or where the soil can be watered or irrigated. As the plants grow the base of the plant begins to swell, and eventually when fully matured a large round bulb is produced about 6 to 10 cm in diameter with long tubular mainly upright green leaves. The matured onions which are usually half immersed in the soil soon ripen in the summer sun becoming quite firm, and with straw to brown coloured skin. It is common practice to break the leafy stem just above the neck of the bulb to encourage ripening and to prevent the plant from flowering and the consequent deterioration of the bulb. If allowed, the onion produces a single stem with a round globular cluster of tiny white flowers eventually producing seed. When the onion bulbs are firm and ripe the onions are lifted, dried and stored in a cool dry place. In this state they will store for several months. Herodotus said that very large amounts of money was expended to provide the builders of the Great Pyramid of Khufu with onions. The variety of onion growing in Egypt is quite mild, sweet, juicy and can be eaten raw.

The onion is a useful vegetable for culinary use, where it is used in cooking to add flavour, just as it was in ancient Egypt. It was valued as a medicinal herb and is still well-regarded today for its properties. The juice extract from the bulb is antibiotic, and helpful in reducing the effects of colds, ejecting phlegm for coughs, and encouraging discharge of urine (diuretic), capable of lowering blood pressure, encouraging

clotting, reducing blood sugar levels. In Pharaonic times, perhaps because of its antibiotic properties, the onion was used in the mummification process. Onion bulbs on their own were used to keep snakes away from human habitations.

Allium porrum

Common Leek
Family: Liliaceae

The leek makes upright growth with a creamy white elongated bulb developing at the base and having dark green leaves. Unlike the onion it does not develop a globular shape when maturing; the stem is straight and becomes thickened, the base of it is usually white or blanched and at least 30 cm in length by 2.5 cm diameter before the broad leaves emerge from it. The blanched part of the stem can be extended by drawing more earth up around the plant as it grows making that part more tender when cooked for eating as a vegetable. When harvested for culinary use the excess leaves are cut off leaving an edible stem about 20 cm in length. The leek was grown in Egypt from ancient times and regarded as a sacred plant. It was featured in tomb paintings. Whether the leek described above is the actual species grown in ancient Egypt is open to conjecture, as in Palestine the salad leek, *Allium kurrat*, was grown, which is smaller with narrower leaves. The common leek and the salad leek are derived from the wild leek, *Allium ampeloprasum.*

The leek was used by the Egyptian Coptic priests as a cure for night blindness when combined with human urine.

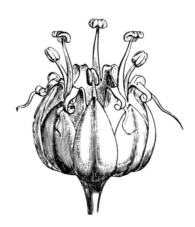

Allium sativum

Garlic
Family: Liliaceae

Garlic was an important part of the ancient Egyptian diet, and was also grown for its medicinal and preservative properties. Garlic was left in tombs as offerings. Easily recognisable bulbs, some with leaves still intact, were found in Tutankhamun's tomb, and are now in the possession of Cairo Museum. The garlic bulb is mainly rounded in shape, and made up of several layers of fleshy scales (cloves), usually creamy white and attached to the main bulb in the centre. The leaves are long, clear green, resembling grass, and the plant eventually produces one flowering stem up to 50 cm high bearing white flowers shaded green, which are sterile. The only way the plant can be propagated is by separating the cloves and planting in the soil individually. Its parentage is unknown and apparently botanists are of the opinion that it probably originated from a wild species in Sumer (now Iran). According to an inscription in an Egyptian pyramid the labourers involved in its building ate vast quantities of garlic, leeks and onion and the costs amounted to sixteen hundred talents of silver. The pyramid required the employment of one hundred thousand men and took thirty years to complete.

Aloe vera

Aloe Vera
Family: Liliaceae

A perennial plant that tends to make rosettes of thick succulent leaves which have a waxy surface and spiky tips, grey-green in colour, speckled with creamy-green striations. It readily forms suckers that eventually  form large clumps of plants growing up to 90 cm in height. Aloe vera produces spikes of tubular flowers in summer which can be yellow, orange or red. The plant is mainly native to south east and north Africa, preferring well drained sandy soils, and will survive desert conditions. It is not certain whether it grew in Egypt — it was possibly an introduction, but something resembling it was painted on two objects found in Tutankhamun's tomb and it is claimed to have been identified in wall paintings. Assuming the identification of *Aloe vera* in ancient Egyptian texts is correct, the Ebers Papyrus, a medical papyrus from 1550 BC, includes a prescription for catarrh which included the sap from the leaves of this plant. It is known that the Coptic Egyptians prescribed aloe for digestive problems and external inflammations. It is interesting to note that it is used for the same disorders today and to treat skin problems such as eczema, burns and scalds. The plant is easily propagated by lifting large clumps and splitting or teasing apart to separate the offsets from the parent plants and re-planting in well drained sandy soils.

Apium graveolens

Wild Celery
Family: Umbelliferae

Wild celery is a biennial herb growing to a height of 30 to 80 cm, tending to thrive in moist places. It has a bulbous fleshy root with broad stalks which are solid and grooved, and lobed pinnate leaves having a distinctive strong smell typical of celery, the wild type having quite a bitter tasting stem not suitable for eating. The cultivated plants have broader stalks, usually milder and good for eating. The flowers are tiny, pale green-white, borne in small-umbels and later developing small brown seeds. Celery was certainly cultivated in Pharaonic Egypt; a garland composed of celery leaves was laid over the mummy of Tutankhamun (*c*.1352 BC). There are other examples dating from around 1000 BC, one garland in particular can be seen in a glass display case in the Agricultural Museum, Cairo. Celery has several applications as a medicinal herb and according to papyrus texts was important in Pharaonic times. The Egyptians of those days certainly used celery to treat human conditions but we don't know what parts of the plant were used. For instance, celery was used to stimulate the appetite, cool the uterus and act as a contraceptive. Today it is used to reduce blood pressure, act as a tonic, relieve indigestion, stimulate the uterus, and is effective as a diuretic, and for conditions such as gout, osteoarthritis and rheumatoid arthritis.

Balanites aegyptiaca

Egyptian Plum
Family: Balanitaceae

In ancient times this native tree grew in the Nile Valley. It is now very scarce in Egypt, but it can be found near the Dead Sea and in Africa. When crushed, the fruit produces Balanos oil which is thought to have been used as an unguent. Some Arabian traders in Jordan are thought to sell the oil as 'Balm of Gilead', though the shrub which produces the genuine balm is *Commiphora gileadensis*. The Egyptian plum is a small evergreen tree growing up to 3 to 4 metres high, usually having a thick trunk with many sharp thorny branches and ovate leaves in pairs, and later greenish-white flowers in the leaf axils. Fruit are formed later which are almost plum-like except that it has a brittle smooth shell changing from green to purple as it ripens. The fruit inside is pulpy with a hard kernel which when crushed produces the light yellow balanos oil.

Cannabis sativa

Hemp
Family: Cannabidaceae

Cannabis is a native of central Asia, central Europe and Russia but was an introduction to Egypt possibly before 2500 BC. It was first mentioned in hieroglyphic texts relating to the pyramids and in papyrus texts, and it was used in herbal medicine and for making rope. The plant can reach a height of 5 metres with finely divided palmate leaves and green flowers in many branched spikes (panicles). In many countries of the world today the growing and possession of this narcotic for eating or smoking is illegal except in parts of Asia and the Middle East. The flowering tops of female plants make the preparation known as marijuana, and resin from female plants called hasheesh is smoked through water pipes.  Ancient Egyptians recognised its medicinal value though so far evidence suggests that they were not aware of the narcotic effects. Several papyrus texts listed its medicinal uses, including the Ramesseum medical papyrus part III where an eye treatment is described consisting of ground celery and hemp mixed together then left outside overnight to gather moisture from the dew. The eyes were bathed with the solution in the early morning. Combined with other ingredients it was applied externally for inflammations, and internally as an enema and for contraction of the uterus. It is beneficial as a laxative and to treat glaucoma. It is interesting to note that the treatments used by the ancient Egyptian physicians have been proved to be valid.

Capparis spinosa "Spinosa" (syn. C. aegyptia)

Caper
Family: Capparaceae

A variable species having four named varieties growing in Egypt: "Spinosa", "Canescens", "Inermis" and "Deserti". This small shrub is commonly known as the Caper in the English language and named spinosa as it has many thorns or sharp spines. The plant was known and used by the ancient Greeks — the Latin name *Capparis* is probably derived from the Greek name 'kapparis'. When found in its natural habitat the plant tends to scramble along the ground or grows as a bush with hanging branches. If grown as a plant cultivated for commercial purposes its habit is more upright, making a bush up to one metre in height. It can be found growing naturally in rock crevices, on steep cliffs or stone walls and in fine sandy soils. Capers are able to withstand salt spray, and can be found growing along sea shores surviving in very dry soils by means of very deep spreading roots. The growth of the plant is not inhibited by fierce sunlight and dry heat which can exceed 40 °C or cold temperatures down to -8 °C. Due to human exploitation

all the variants of this plant in the wild are threatened with extinction, though growing in cultivated areas is a means of guaranteeing its survival. In Egypt the wild plant grows in the desert, oases and Sinai, and it is widespread in the Middle East, Arabia and Asia.

The plant has woody stems which often branch out near ground level, tending to be pendulous with many sharp spines. The leaves can vary, but are often ovate and tend to be almost round or elliptical and from 1 to 4 cm in length, usually grey-green or blue-green. Leaf texture can be shiny and smooth or covered in tiny hairs, tending to be

hard and fleshy, having short stems with two sharp spines at the base. Sometimes *Capparis spinosa* has leaves with sharp spines at their apex. The flowers last up to two days and appear between March and June on the previous years growth. They are about 4 to 5 cm in diameter, emerging from the leaf axils with four white petals and many stamen filaments, usually white but sometimes pink. Later, fruits develop which at first are green, becoming red when ripe, hanging down like an elongated pear shape up to 5 cm long, 1.5 cm in diameter. The fruit pods contain numerous tiny blackish-brown seeds.

Whether the ancient Egyptians were aware of this plant and its properties is not certain, but the ancient Greeks must have been familiar with it as Dioscorides wrote about its medicinal use. Queen Cleopatra VII was said to have served food to Caesar spiced with capers. Flower buds are gathered from the plant when they are green and in tight bud, and are pickled in vinegar. There is a worldwide demand for them and they are popular for their piquant flavour. They are often added to food in the Mediterranean region. The caper plant is now regarded as a valuable crop, sold in Egypt and for export abroad, and because of increased demand the need for its commercial cultivation has become essential. In the not so distant past *Capparis spinosa* was common in Egypt growing as a wild plant, and it is probable that the native people of Egypt had sufficient supplies without needing to cultivate it.

Like many medicinal herbs the stems and leaves can be stored when dried without losing its beneficial properties, and the prunings from the cultivated shrubs are utilised in this way. Various parts of this herb have been traditionally used by native people for its medicinal properties. It is said to be effective in encouraging discharge of urine, and may be used to treat liver diseases, ulcers, gout, rheumatism, fevers, headaches and toothache for example.

To increase stocks for cultivation seeds should ideally be gathered as soon as possible after ripening and sown straight away. If the seeds are allowed to dry out, which does not take long in the dry heat, dormancy sets in which can only be overcome by soaking in warm water and refrigeration for 3 months. Sow in trays in a peat or peat substitute compost with gritty sand added to improve drainage and firm lightly. Cover seed with loose riddled compost and keep moist in a greenhouse at a temperature of 18–20 °C. Prick out seedlings into small pots when large enough to handle, eventually planting out during winter or early spring. It can take up to four years before the plants produce optimum yields, which are obtained by pruning every winter to encourage flower buds on first year growth. Young plants can also be produced from firm stem cuttings rooted in a propagating case having been dipped in a rooting hormone with bottom heat of 18–21°C. With this method the capers will be giving good yields in three years.

Carthamnus tinctorius

Safflower
Family: Compositae

Also known as saffron thistle and false saffron, safflower is an annual herb, growing up to a metre in height, with erect stems and toothed leaves bearing sharp spines. As it is a member of the daisy family it has a composite head of flower composed of many yellow-orange florets with spiny sepals having some resemblance to a thistle. The florets produce a pigment which is both yellow and red — when added to water the solution turns yellow, but when added to alcohol a permanent red dye is produced for dyeing fabrics. The plant is thought to be a native of Egypt, and was introduced into Europe from there in the sixteenth century. The ancient Egyptians were known to have used the safflower for dyeing mummy wrappings, and for pressing the seeds to produce oil.

Today the safflower is grown as a crop mainly for its valuable cooking oil which is reputed to reduce cholesterol levels. It is also used to treat coronary artery disease, jaundice, measles and menstrual problems. The safflower is grown from seed in spring, and prefers dry sandy soils in full sun.

91

Cedrus libani

Cedar of Lebanon
Family: Pinaceae

A well-known tree originating from western Asia, particularly Lebanon, and north west Africa. Makes a large impressive tree, some specimens capable of reaching to 40 metres with wide spreading branches. Young trees are mainly conical in shape, but as the tree matures it becomes more flat topped and branches become tiered with lower ones being horizontal. The needle-like leaves are green to greyish-green, sometimes blue-grey, about 2 to 3.5 cm in length. Produces barrel shaped cones 8 to 10 cm long which take two years to mature, at which point they shatter and spread their seeds. The ancient Egyptians imported the timber of this species of cedar from Mount Lebanon for use in building, reputedly from the 4th Dynasty. It was said to be used in the construction of Cheops' boat that was discovered in a pit at the side of the Great Pyramid in Giza. Although in a dismantled state when found, a conservator was able to completely re-build the boat which can now be viewed in a building at the site. Cedar wood is reddish brown in colour, and exudes a fragrant sap or gum when first cut. This acts as a natural preservative, which is why it is so long lasting. Wood boring insect larvae do not attack the timber, and it is easy to fashion by hand compared with other woods. The Egyptians extracted oil from the tree for use in embalming, but the oil does not appear to be used for any other purpose. Today, the oil is used to treat skin diseases, as a fungicide, an antiseptic, an insect repellent and as an inhalant for bronchitis. Cedar wood is still used in joinery, such as for the construction of small greenhouses and outdoor furniture, as it does not need wood preservative. The wood does lose its reddish colour, however, fading until it has a silvery hue, and thus needs a clear preservative to retain its colour. Propagation of the tree is by seed sown in spring in a seedbed containing a high content of leaf mould, particularly from well-rotted pine needles.

Centaurea depressa

Cornflower
Family: Compositae

This species of cornflower is grown as a cultivated plant in the Middle East and in Egypt it featured in tomb paintings, sometimes incorporated into garlands for mummies and decorating funeral coffins. This herb is an annual having several strong wiry stems growing up to 40 cm high with lanceolate almost linear leaves directly attached to the stem and grey in colour. At the end of each stem are bright-blue flowers which resemble thistle heads. It is not certain what medicinal value the plant had in the Pharaonic period of Egypt as it has not been identified in papyrus texts. As a medicinal herb in modern times it is used for conjunctivitis, as an eye tonic, and for mouth ulcers. It prefers well drained soils and can be propagated from seed sown in spring or autumn.

Ceratonia siliqua

Carob Tree or Locust Bean Tree
Family: Leguminosae

The carob tree is indigenous to the Mediterranean region, and was traditionally grown mainly for the seed pods which provided food for livestock. It makes a medium-sized broad-headed tree up to 9 metres high and 10 metres spread and a heavy trunk with a tendency to be hollow. It is an evergreen bearing dark green pinnate leaves often without a terminal leaflet. The leaves are arranged alternately on the young shoots, each one up to 20 cm long. They have a leathery smooth texture, slightly shiny upper side with new growths that are pale purple. The flowers are very small and inconspicuous, mainly green with a slight red tint, borne like catkins on old wood. During spring and summer, green fruit pods develop which resemble runner beans, although not quite as long when mature, and either straight or curved. The beans are evenly distributed in the pod which are thickened where beans are present. The pods turn brown in late summer and autumn but the flesh is quite hard, perhaps a bit too hard for human consumption but ideal for cattle feed. The tree develops a very deep root system and adapts very well to drought conditions lasting for many months which is common in Mediterranean regions. Like all members of the legume family it has a root system which is host to nitrogen fixing bacteria. The bacteria absorb nitrogen from the atmosphere and attach to the roots in the form of nodules that contain nitrates, which are beneficial to the tree.

The Bible says that John the Baptist, while in the desert, ate the pods from this tree; hence it is called St John's Bread. The flesh is quite sweet and nutritious and similar to sweetened cocoa. Combined with saturated fats it produces a sweet confection that is almost like chocolate in flavour and texture, and the way it melts in the mouth, and in this form is simply called Carob.

The seed when ripe is used for its gum as a thickening agent. This characteristic makes it a useful medicine for diarrhoea as it has a binding effect. It is also taken for the soothing of the digestive system.

In ancient times a standard of weight measurement was adopted for the weighing of precious gem stones such as diamonds and gold which was based on carob seeds. One carob seed represented one "carat" unit and in more recent times it was decided that one carat unit was equal to 0.2 grams.

Cicer arietinum

Chick Pea
Family: Leguminosae

A member of the pea family, the chick pea is an annual plant growing up to 20 cm in height, usually erect, and having pinnate toothed leaves. The flowers are tiny, either blue or white, later developing a one or two seeded pod which has a distinctive shape, hence its other common names, ram's-head and falcon-head. A model granary that was found in Tutankhamun's tomb contained cereal seeds and a few chick pea seeds, and papyrus texts dating from the 18th Dynasty indicate that it grew in Egypt.

Today in Egypt the seeds are crushed and mixed with sesame seed and olive oil to produce a paste called hummus, often eaten with bread. Sometimes spice is added to it for flavour.

Cichorium intybus

Chicory
Family: Compositae

Chicory is a perennial, native to Europe, Western Asia and North Africa, including Egypt. It usually makes a tall plant up to 1.5 metres, having spirally arranged lanceolate and toothed leaves partly enclosing the stems. The flowers appear in clusters in the upper leaf axils of the plant, similar in appearance to a dandelion but having blue flowers. Chicory produces a stout tap root which is used today as a coffee substitute when roasted. It is also a constituent of herbal medicines. The roots and leaves are used as a diuretic, a laxative and to treat liver complaints, rheumatism, gout and haemorrhoids. There is another type of chicory used for salads known as Witloof, which looks similar to the conical heart of a small cos lettuce.

Citrullus colocynthus

Colocynth or Bitter Apple
Family: Cucurbitaceae

This plant is indigenous in Egypt, growing in the desert and believed to be the parent plant from which the watermelon was derived. It has a creeping habit producing long trailing perennial branches which develop round fruits about the size of a medium sized apple when mature. As the fleshy fruits are developing they are dark green, sometimes mottled, and when ripe become yellow. The fruits are very bitter and highly toxic, causing severe bowel disorders if eaten. Interpreters of ancient Egyptian papyrus texts have so far been unable to reliably identify this plant, so its medicinal use is unknown for that period. This is not to say that they were not aware of its medicinal properties; today it is used medicinally to treat dizziness, headaches, neuralgia, stomach pain combined with nausea and vomiting, kidney or ovary pain, sciatica, gout, rheumatism and lower abdominal pains sometimes associated with diarrhoea.

Citrullus Lanatus (syn. *C. vulgaris*)

Water Melon
Family: Cucurbitaceae

An annual plant grown in irrigated land beside the Nile which flourishes in the dry heat. Its fruit was an important food for the poor people of ancient Egypt. The plant produces long trailing shoots which scramble along the ground bearing long lobed hairy leaves larger than the human hand. As these shoots grow, yellow flowers develop. As they shrivel, the embryonic fruit starts to swell, eventually becoming larger than a football. When the fruit is ripe it has a hard dark green skin often speckled with yellow dots, and reddish-pink succulent flesh. The pulpy flesh is juicy and fairly sweet containing several dark almost black seeds scattered throughout the fruit. It is stated in the Bible (Numbers 11.4–10) that the Israelites missed eating the thirst quenching Melons and Cucumbers after they were exiled from Egypt and could not eat anything except for manna.

Two baskets were found in Tutankhamun's tomb which contained well preserved water melon seeds, which would have been eaten lightly roasted.

The plant originates from Africa and is believed to be the result of plant breeding by African tribes that adopted early agricultural cropping systems. It is thought to be closely related by parentage to the colocynth (*Citrullus colocynthis*) which grows in the Egyptian deserts and in the drier parts of Africa. The colocynth has round yellow fruits about 10 cm in diameter which are poisonous.

Commiphora gileadensis (syn. *Balsamodendron opobalsamum*)

Balm of Gilead
Family: Burseraceae

This shrub is deciduous. In fact, it remains leafless for most of the year until after the rainy season, and then holds its leaves only for a short while. The small leaves are borne in pairs close to the thin thornless stems and are compound in form with three simple leaflets. During this short growing period the four-petalled flowers are produced in the leaf axils, followed by berries. In order to obtain the sticky resinous balm, incisions have to be made in the bark. Later, the hardened lumps of resin are collected just like myrrh, which is a related species. It is a native of south-west Asia, and possibly in a part of Jordan that was called Gilead in ancient times. In the Bible, Jeremiah made the well-known remark: "Is there no balm in Gilead" (Jeremiah 8.22).

In a recipe mentioned by Dioscorides (11.91) the ancient Egyptians used *Balsamodendron opobalsamum* as a thickening agent in scented goose or pork fat. This suggests that it was available to the Egyptians like myrrh, but was brought in from Asia.

Coriandrum sativum

Coriander
Family: Umbelliferae

Coriander is an annual herb indigenous to Egypt, north Africa and south west Asia, but is now cultivated virtually worldwide. Coriander has been grown in Egypt since ancient times, and the earliest evidence comes from seeds surprisingly well preserved in Tutankhamun's tomb. It is related to parsley, with lower leaves which resemble the large flat-leaved variety of parsley, though the leaves higher up the stem are very finely divided and almost insignificant. The plant grows up to 60 cm high with thin stems and white or mauve flowers in small clusters or umbels. Later, seeds are formed within a hard ribbed fruit case which has a fragrant aroma. The seeds have a sharp spicy flavour appreciated as an ingredient in curries, pickles and for seasoning meats. Oil is extracted from the seeds which is used medicinally and for perfumes, and the leaves contain the same oil and are used in cooking for flavour. The oil is beneficial for the digestive system, helping to improve the appetite and having bactericidal and fungicidal proper-ties. In ancient times Pliny expressed the opinion that the best quality coriander came from Egypt. He also said that when combined with honey or raisins it healed spreading sores, diseased testes, burns, carbuncles, and sore ears. Eye fluxes could also be treated by adding woman's milk as a base medium and applying externally.

Coriander is grown from seed sown in January in Egypt as it needs cool, damp conditions to allow the ger-minated seedlings to establish. If the soil is too dry at the seedling stage there is a tendency for it to bolt or pro-duce flowers prematurely. Later on when well established it prefers hot, dry conditions and well drained soil in full sun.

Cucumis milo

Snake Cucumber
Family: Cucurbitaceae

This is not the cucumber we are familiar with in Britain, which is *Cucumis sativa*, but a variety of musk-melon that is not as broad and perhaps half the length of *C. sativa*, curved like a short snake, and grooved along its length. Like the melon it has long scrambling stems growing along the ground having broad entire five-sided leaves and small female or male yellow flowers (female flowers have embryo fruit already forming). It has been grown in Egypt since ancient times, and can still be found for sale in the markets and vegetable shops in Spain and other Mediterranean countries. The Hebrews, when they were exiled in Egypt,

were familiar with this vegetable but when they left and found themselves in the wilderness they missed the juicy fruits: "...and the children of Israel also wept again, and said, Who shall give us flesh to eat? We remember the fish, which we did eat in Egypt freely; the cucumbers, and melons, and the leeks ... But now our soul is dried away..." (Numbers 11.4–6).

In the papyrus documents from Egypt, identification of the cucumber is uncertain, although carvings and wall paintings in tombs show that they were available then. The British Museum displayed an Egyptian wooden box with hinged lid in the shape of a snake cucumber with grooved sides. There is no information as to whether the Egyptians used the fruit for medicinal purposes.

Today the fruit of the cucumber is used as a herbal medicine for heat rashes, sunburn, scalds and conjunctivitis.

Cyperus papyrus

Papyrus
Family: Cyperaceae

The plant grows best in shallow still water at the edge of marshes with its tuberous horizontal roots spreading into the mud. It produces stems which are triangular and in ideal conditions can be from 5 to 7 cm in cross section and reach a height of 5 metres. The base of the stem is protected by short brown leaves, and when the plant is fully grown it produces umbels of brown flowers at the top of the stem, though initially the head appears to be a mass of fine grasses varying from 8 to 15 cm in length.

The plant has an unusual way of reproducing itself. Maybe due to the weight of the flower head, the stem begins to bend over, and the umbel eventually becoming submerged in the water. In a short while

new shoots begin to grow from underneath and roots develop from the upper surface of the umbel. Once the new green shoots emerge from the water it is a sign that it is well established and the old stem withers and dies. The papyrus can be propagated by division of the roots, and even if the stems are harvested new shoots will emerge from the roots. The plant's ability to renew itself is probably the reason the Papyrus came to be associated symbolically with resurrection or rebirth. This could also be why bunches of papyrus were brought as funerary offerings, together with food and drink, to rejuvenate the reborn Pharaoh when he visited his tomb.

During the times of the Pharaohs the papyrus flourished as a wild or indigenous plant which grew in the marshy areas of the Nile delta in the north of Egypt. Today the plant cannot be found in Egypt due to silting and draining of the delta for the cultivation of crops. It can now only be found growing wild in the White Nile in Sudan and Ethiopia. The papyrus can also be found flourishing in the Syracuse area of Sicily and is believed to have been introduced from Egypt by the Greeks or Romans. In Ancient Egypt the plant was used for rope making, basketry, and even boat construction, and it was recognised as an ideal writing material. The English word 'paper' is believed to be a direct derivation of papyrus. It is known that the use of this writing material goes back to about 3000 BC, as evidenced by the discovery of a blank roll found in the tomb of an official known as Hemaka in the reign of King Den. Even though it is a fragile material which could easily have disintegrated after so long, numerous samples have survived to the present day due to the very dry climate of Egypt. The manufacture of papyrus seems to have been a monopoly of Egypt, though its use as writing material spread into Palestine and other middle eastern countries. Today the plant is grown commercially in a few suitable places in northern Egypt, mainly to provide for the tourists wanting to purchase papyrus showing hieroglyphic script and illustration.

The manufacture of papyrus writing material begins with the harvesting of the mature stems between June and September. The thinner

part of the stem below the flower head is discarded in favour of the lower part of the stem, where the greater density of the pith is more stable and more suitable for the purpose. The stem is then cut into lengths that depend on the size of sheet required, and the outer rind is removed leaving a white pith. The remaining stem is then cut lengthwise into strips and soaked in water. The strips are laid horizontally on a flat board, then another layer is laid at right angles to cover the lower layer. The two layers are bonded together by placing them in a press, and the resulting sheet is allowed to dry. The sap of the plant contains gums which glue the layers together when heavily pressed. Several sheets were often glued together to produce scrolls of rolled up sheets which made them easy to carry. It is not certain what the Egyptians used as a pen for writing, but the Romans used reeds sharpened to a point at one end to produce a nib with a small split like the metal nibs of the twentieth century.

Many papyri have been found in the tombs of Pharaohs and important officials, and have often been discovered in mummy coffins and contained within the mummy wrappings. The 'Great Harris Papyrus' of Rameses III is the longest papyrus scroll ever found in Egypt, at 42 metres long. It is thought that some scrolls mentioned in the Bible might have been made of papyrus, parchment or vellum. Jeremiah was asked by the Lord to write his commands on a scroll (Jeremiah 36:2), and in a synagogue on the day of the Sabbath, Jesus was handed a scroll from the prophet Isaiah (Luke 4:16-20).

The world's largest collection of papyri can be found in the British Museum, safely stored in glass display cabinets in a room entirely devoted to Papyrus. A lot of information about the lives of Egyptians in ancient times has been learned from Papyri.

The illustrations of papyrus carved on the walls of tombs and temples often show the plant as a clump of tall stems with almost fan shaped heads. Papyrus marshes are represented by several clumps or a thicket of papyrus, and are symbolically a place where the deceased Pharaoh could go hunting in the eternal afterlife. The papyrus marshes

provided an ideal habitat for the ducks and geese that were hunted by the local peasants and noblemen alike as a source of food. The decorative chest found in King Tutankhamun's tomb features one panel showing the King hunting in papyrus marshes with a bow and arrow, aiming at the wildfowl fluttering above, and with his Queen sitting and holding an arrow.

The well-known painting on plaster, 'Fowling in the Marshes', was taken from the tomb of Nebamun and transferred onto the wall of a mock tomb in the British Museum. On the left of the picture is a papyrus thicket with various species of birds, including ducks and geese, both perched and flying above it. In the centre, Nebamun stands in a papyrus boat with a throw stick (similar to a boomerang) in his left hand and three birds in his right hand. The bottom left corner shows part of a spear which has penetrated a fish in the water. The drawing of the birds and fish and the colouring is very realistic, and some of the species are recognisable. Nebamun may have been an important official or nobleman of Amenhotep III or Amenhotep IV, during the 18th Dynasty, from Thebes.

A similar theme is a hunting scene in the tomb of King Ay (1327–1323 BC) which appears to be a feature in noblemen's tombs only. Gardens featured in tomb paintings often included pools containing large clumps of papyrus. In fact, Queen Hatshepsut's mortuary temple at Deir el-Bahri has two empty T-shaped pools in which the remains of papyrus were found by archaeologists.

In the Egyptian tradition, carvings in relief inside tombs and temples of papyrus thickets tended to be shown as if on a mound above the surrounding water. This theme was symbolic of the land rising above the waters when the world was created and the god Nun emerged. The symbolism connected with the papyrus influenced the architecture of temple buildings; the pillared (hypostyle) halls were constructed so that the columns represented papyrus marshes. The cylindrical columns had a distinctive shape usually curving inwards at the base before widening to a plinth, and tapering towards the bell-shaped capital (imitating the open umbel of the plant). The aisles between the columns represented the waters surrounding the mound, leading to higher ground which represented the god's sanctuary. There is a good example of a huge papyrus-column, the only remaining one erected by Taharqa, in the first court at Karnak. Some of the earliest examples of stone pillars following a similar theme are those to be found against the remaining

walls of the temple near to Djoser's Five Step Pyramid at Saqqara. These columns are quite slender compared with those mentioned earlier and have triangular stems, probably meant to be more decorative than supporting. Archaeological evidence suggests that it was quite common for the bases of papyrus columns to have representations of the basal leaves painted onto the stone in stripes of red, green and blue.

Triangular stemmed papyrus columns at Saqqara.

107

Ficus carica

Common Fig
Family: Moraceae

The edible or common fig (*Ficus carica*) is a close relative of the sycomore fig. The tree is thought to originate from Caria, Asia Minor, hence the specific name 'carica', but is well suited to the Mediterranean climate. Evidence of its cultivation goes back to Neolithic times. Nine charred figs were discovered during an archaeological excavation north of the ancient city of Jericho and found to be 11,400 years old. The tree featured quite often in the bible and its first mention is in Genesis in relation to the story of Adam and Eve: "The eyes of both of them were opened, and they realised that they were naked; so they sewed fig leaves together and made coverings for themselves." In the art world, particularly in Europe in the past few hundred years, there have been periods where for the sake of propriety nudes portrayed in paintings have their private parts covered with the fig leaf.

The leaves of the common fig are mainly palmate which divide into five lobes often being described as hand shaped. They are usually a little longer than the human hand and are a glossy dark green above, and pale green and slightly hairy underneath. In the more northern parts of the Mediterranean the tree loses its leaves in the winter. All members of the genus *Ficus* exude a white milky sap if a leaf or branch is broken off or fractured.

The ripe figs are pear-shaped, sweet to the taste and fleshy, about the same size as a kiwi fruit and either purple or a yellowish-green. Like the sycomore fig the fruit is an enlarged hollow receptacle containing numerous fruitlets called a syconium.

In order to produce fruit the wild varieties are pollinated by a wasp which is specific to the tree; it is a symbiotic relationship and one cannot survive without the other. The flowers are inside the receptacle and the wasp has to enter it in the same way as for the sycomore fig, through a small hole in the apex. However, it differs from the sycamore fig in that it produces caprifigs before the onset of winter which contain infertile female flowers and eggs laid by the female wasps. As the warmer weather comes the eggs hatch and after mating the winged female wasps leave the caprifigs which do not swell as they are infertile. By the time the wasps leave the tree a crop of new flower receptacles are available which contain fertile female flowers. Before the female wasps emerge from the caprifigs their bodies brush against the fertile male flowers containing ripe pollen. This pollen is transferred to new spring syconiums when the wasps penetrate them causing pollination and in a short while producing swollen ripe figs. The common fig usually has two crops per year with a first crop in spring produced

on the previous years growth and a second crop in late summer on the current years growth.

The characteristics of the common fig in relation to its use in ancient Egyptian medicines is very similar to the sycomore fig. Its use as a laxative was well known although it was usually combined with milk and sweet beer.

Ficus sycomorus

Sycomore Fig
Family: Moraceae

The sycomore fig (*Ficus sycomorus*) is a member of the Moraceae family, and has unusual characteristics, some of which are shared with the mulberry, a member of the same family; it is sometimes called the mulberry fig. The tree is a native of tropical Africa, where it is known as "The Queen of Trees" possibly because of its ability to provide a livelihood for a wide range of insects and animals. In Egypt, evidence suggests that the tree was known from the 1st Dynasty, probably introduced to provide shade and fruit.

Sycomore fig makes a substantial wide spreading tree at least 15 metres in height, and even reaching 30 metres in a tropical forest, often having several large branches emerging from a massive trunk near the ground. The leaves have a rough surface, leathery and heart-shaped, and normally evergreen in warm climates; it is only in cooler regions where it drops most of its leaves in winter. If the leaves are cut or fractured they exude a milky white sap or latex similar to the substance that comes from the rubber plant (*Ficus elastica*) to which it is related. The latex in the mid ribs and side ribs of the leaf is inedible or poisonous to various leaf sucking and nibbling insects and restricts their activity, thus protecting the tree.

The sycomore fig is capable of providing fruit virtually throughout the year. The fruits are oval and up to 2.5 cm in diameter when ripe, smaller than the common fig (*Ficus carica*) and borne in large clusters on short stems spread throughout the branches of the tree.

The fruit develops in a green receptacle known as a syconium which contains a central cavity lined with very tiny florets and a small opening at the tip of the embryonic fruit case. Fertilisation of the fruit is entirely dependent on the fig wasp, which penetrates the opening surrounded by male flowers that dust the insect with pollen. Once inside

the cavity the wasp crawls among the female flowers which receive a dusting of pollen, thus completing the process of fertilisation. At the same time, the wasp lays eggs among the flowers. After fertilisation the fruits swell rapidly, becoming ripe in approximately five weeks, which coincides with the wasps emerging from the fruit. Before the winged females emerge they mate with the wingless males who then die inside the cavity having served their purpose. From the time that the winged females leave the ripe fruit they live for no more than twelve hours, in which time they have to find and fertilise flowering figs.

The ripe fruit is inedible for humans unless the fruit is harvested when at an early stage of ripening. Normally the Egyptians climbed the trees in order to obtain suitable fruit for eating. Early harvesting prevents the wasps from reaching the adult stage — if left to develop naturally the dead male wasps remaining in the ripe fruit makes them unpalatable. It is unlikely that all the fruits would be cut as they are produced so prolifically and some would be out of reach, allowing the beneficial life-cycle of the wasps to continue. According to F. Nigel Hepper, research carried out during the latter part of the twentieth century reached the conclusion that ripening of the fruit occurs in a matter of a few days if the syconium's outer surface is cut, and prevents the continuation of the life-cycle of the wasp.

Where the sycomore fig grows in tropical Africa it attracts many birds and other animals because of the abundance of fruits. The animals that eat the fruit disperse the seeds which then readily germinate in moist soil. In Egypt, where rainfall except in the Nile Delta is a very rare event, natural germination of fig seeds is unlikely.

It is a matter for conjecture as to how the sycomore came to be introduced into Egypt in the first place; maybe traders from Africa brought the fruit in dried form. Tomb gardeners or estate workers could have extracted the seeds from the dried fruit and germinated them in irrigated nursery beds, growing them on until they were large enough for transplanting into their permanent positions.

The sycomore figs in Egypt make massive trees and are capable of reaching a great age. In ancient times they provided timber for the making of sarcophagi (coffins) and for general woodworking, and it is frequently discovered in temples. Although a soft wood, many examples still exist which are at least 3,000 years old.

The sycomore is regarded as important in Egyptian mythology and frequently featured in tomb paintings. The tree represents the goddesses Nut and Hathor who were shown on walls of tombs as if being incorporated into the tree. Hathor was called the "Lady of the Sycomore" and depicted as offering sustenance to the deceased in the form of food and water. This association with the sycomore is one of the reasons why it was planted near tombs. The Pharaoh Mentuhotep I (2061–2010 BC) had sycomore trees planted along each side of the ramp leading up to his temple at Deir el-Bahri.

In Pharaonic times the ripened fruit of the sycomore was a very useful ingredient in many herbal medicines. The fig on its own was known as an effective laxative although Lise Manniche in her *Ancient Egyptian Herbal* suggests a combination of figs, cow's milk and honey in equal parts was administered for this purpose. It was used in medicines for the treatment of asthma and toothache, and dry unripe fruits were used to kill worm in the digestive tract. The sap of the tree was used in medicine and obtained by penetrating the bark of its main trunk in early spring with a sharp stone and allowing it to dry into a granular crystal form. These granules were kept dry in a vase and melted when required for applying to tumours. This apparently eliminated any pain eventually leading to reduction of tumours or swellings on the surface of the skin and possibly their complete disappearance. However, information concerning the curing of skin ailments and tumours is not entirely clear. Lise Manniche states that the latex in the sap of the tree irritates the skin, and juice squeezed from the fruit may have been used instead.

Hordeum vulgare

Barley
Family: Gramineae

Barley is an annual grass which is not as tall growing as wheat and will tolerate dryer, poorer soils. It has longer more whiskery flower heads than wheat, which are held slightly below the horizontal. It has a lower protein content per grain than wheat, but it is grown more frequently in Egypt and Israel for bread making. *Hordeum vulgare* species is known as "six rowed barley" with three rows of grain on each side of the head. A primitive "two rowed barley" *Hordeum distlichon* was discovered during excavations of Stone Age dwellings and both forms have been found in Egyptian tombs. The crop was usually sown in October and November, and ready to harvest in February. In favourable areas a second sowing was made in February for harvesting in June. The method of harvesting, threshing and winnowing was the same as for wheat (*triticum dicoccum*).

Hyphaene thebaica

Doum Palm
Family: Arecaceae

The doum or dom palm used to be a native of the Nile valley and now grows in Upper Egypt and Sudan. A typical characteristic of this palm is that the trunk tends to divide low down, often having two or more stems, unlike the date palm which only has one stem. Like most palms the leaves are concentrated at the top of a bare stem and in this case are fan-shaped. The fruits are carried in clusters on short stems close to the trunk and among the leaves. They are oval in shape and up to 8 cm in length, having a smooth skin protecting a very sweet fibrous edible layer surrounding a nut containing a sweet juice. Doum palm fruits have often been found in tombs for pharaohs to enjoy in their after-life; several hundred were found in Rameses III's tomb. The palm is featured in some tomb paintings, particularly in illustrations of tomb gardens. Leaves were often used when dried for basket weaving and rope making.

Lactuca sativa

Cos Lettuce
Family: Compositae

The growing of cos Lettuce goes back to ancient times and is featured in tomb paintings. Cos lettuce is still being grown for eating in Egypt today. It may have been derived from *Lactuca virosa* (wild or great lettuce) which was also available for medicinal use. This lettuce contains latex in the form of mildly narcotic compounds which become more concentrated when the plants are in flower; known as "lactucarium" and sometimes as "lettuce opium", it was used in medical practice in the eighteenth century as a mild sedative that is non-addictive. Cos lettuce was sacred to Min, god of fertility, because of its milky juice which is reminiscent of semen. It was also related to the god Seth: he became pregnant after eating lettuces on which had been scattered the semen of his rival, the god Horus. Priests in the temples were expected to be celibate, which is why priests in the temple of Philae were forbidden to eat lettuce. In ancient Egypt the lettuce was used as a cough suppressant, a mild sedative, and combined with other ingredients as a pain killer and laxative. As a herbal medicine today it is used for insomnia, dry cough, whooping cough, bronchitis and rheumatic pain. It is propagated by seed sown in autumn.

Lawsonia inermis

Henna
Family: Lythraecae

This evergreen shrub is sometimes called mignonette tree or Egyptian privet. It is native to north Africa and south western Asia, and can still be found growing in Egypt. It grows up to 6 metres high, tending to be spindly with thorns and having almost oblong leaves. The flowers are mainly white, sometimes shaded pink, in panicles, and sweetly scented. In the Bible the shrub was called 'camphire'. The Greek physician Dioscorides claimed that the henna grown at Canopus in the Delta was among the best (1.124).

In ancient Egypt it was used as a dye for hair and cloth, and for painting nails. Dark-skinned Nubian women used it to dye their skin a different colour. The Egyptians certainly painted their nails, as shown by mummy evidence. Some also had dyed red hair though there is some dispute as to whether henna was used. The dried leaves of the plant are powdered and small amounts of water added to make a paste which produces an orange-red dye which these days is mainly used as a hair dye though it does have some medicinal value. The identification of this plant in papyrus is not certain but if it is correct it was used as a remedy for loss of hair in ancient Egypt. Today it is used medicinally for skin diseases (including leprosy), wounds, ulcers and herpes.

Henna can be propagated from seed, soft wood cuttings when in active growth, or hardwood cuttings in winter. It prefers well drained sandy soil and needs to be grown in full sun.

Lens culinaris

Lentil
Family: Leguminosae

The cultivation of this crop goes back to the dawn of agriculture and it was widely grown in Egypt during the Pharaonic period. Black carbonised remains of lentils have frequently been found in Egypt during excavations of tombs, including that of Tutankhamun. It is an annual which is similar to the Common Vetch (*Vicia sativa*) making quite slender growth having pinnate leaves with tendrils at their leaf ends. When grown close together the plants grow into a tangled mass up to 25 cm high as the tendrils twine together. They have tiny blue flowers which eventually result in the creation of flat pods containing two seeds up to 6 mm in diameter. The seeds are reddish brown when ripe and split into two equal parts, each part shaped like a convex magnifying glass, which takes its name from the lentil's Latin name 'Lens'. The seeds are greatly valued by the peasants for their high protein content and lentils are capable of growing on poorer soils. Often the peasants combined the pulse with wheat or barley grain to make bread.

Lilium candidum

White or Madonna Lily
Family: Liliaceae

The Madonna lily was grown in ancient Egypt for its perfume. It was probably a late introduction from the eastern Mediterranean. Some wall paintings of labourers picking lily flowers for perfume were found in tombs; one such painting from the 26th Dynasty is preserved in the Louvre, Paris. The lily is a perennial that has scaly bulbs which in Egypt start to grow in the winter, producing a few tufts of leaf to begin with, later producing a flower stem at least 1 metre in height with numerous lance shaped leaves up to 7 cm in length, usually becoming smaller towards the point where the flower buds are formed. The plant, depending on its vigour or growing conditions, can have from 5 to 20 trumpet shaped scented flowers in summer which are pure white except for the inside being yellow at the base with yellow anthers. The Madonna lily does have some medicinal benefits but there is no evidence of its use for this purpose in Pharaonic times. Today it is used for skin problems such as abscesses, burns, chilblains, and alopecia.

Propagation can be achieved by sowing seeds in autumn, or by planting bulb scales and offsets.

Linum usitatissimum

Flax
Family: Linaceae

The flax plant is an annual which grows to a height of almost 1 metre, bearing narrow leaves which are attached to lightly stemmed branches and arranged opposite to each other or alternately. The plant is quite dainty in appearance, fairly narrow in spread, upright, having attractive five-petalled flowers which are pale blue with a violet blotch at the base of its petals. Since ancient times the flax has been grown for the textile known as linen. It is probable that Pharaonic Egypt was the earliest civilisation to use it mainly for clothing, although archaeological evidence suggests that Neolithic man may have used it in this way, too. To produce suitable growth for making into textile fibres, the seeds of the crop are sown thickly so that thin stemmed plants are grown.

When the plant begins to turn yellow at the base of the stem the crop is pulled up by the roots and laid out to dry. Once dry, the stems are soaked in water for at least a week, allowing bacterial action which makes it easier to separate the fibres from the internal part of the hard

central core. This process is called "retting". The stems are left to dry out again on a clean surface, and then the fibres can be separated into threads and combed out ready for spinning and weaving. In ancient times Egypt was noted for its fine quality linen; in the Bible it was said that Moses considered Egyptian linen to be superior. Egypt was also the major source of flax. There were different qualities, the coarser fibres used for ropes and sails were made of linen. Some mummy cloths used for wrapping the dead pharaohs, his relations and officials were made of linen.

The variety used for the production of linseed oil is given more space to branch out and encourage flowering.

Linseed oil is extracted from the seed produced after flowering. The seeds are contained in a five-chambered receptacle and have two flat shiny seeds to each chamber. When grown for the flax fibres, seeds are sown late October for harvesting the following April or May. This has been the practice since ancient times as a later crop would perish in the extreme heat.

Mandragora officinarum

Mandrake, Devil's Apples
Family: Solanaceae

Mandrake is related to the potato, tobacco and deadly nightshade group of plants. Like all plants in this group it has narcotic properties and is slightly poisonous. It is sometimes called "The Love Apple" because it has been used as an aphrodisiac and is well known as an ingredient in love potions, but this idea is probably based on superstition. Mandrake is mentioned in the Bible (Genesis 30) where it was gathered for Rachel, who was childless by Leah's son Reuben, to encourage fertility.

The mandrake is a perennial which develops tap roots that can penetrate several metres in the search for moisture. The root growth is similar to sugar beet and often forked and contorted in such a way as to resemble the lower parts of the human body, which gives rise to its superstitious reputation. The plant produces a rosette of crinkled leaves on the soil surface that are up to 30 cm in length and up to 10 cm wide and deeply veined. Flowers emerge from the centre of the rosette during autumn and winter, each one carried on a short stalk. They are mainly pale mauve, and sometimes greenish-yellow. In spring, fleshy yellow fruits are produced about 2 cm long and broadly pear shaped with a prominent calyx protecting the base. The fruit has an unusual smell similar to an apple and tastes fairly sweet, but if consumed in sufficient quantity can have a narcotic effect causing hallucinations. It is commonly found growing wild in uncultivated or abandoned ground mainly in regions bordering the Mediterranean. It was introduced into Egypt in the New Kingdom, though in its native habitat the plant needed winter rains and so required irrigation in order to grow successfully in Egypt.

From the 18th Dynasty the mandrake featured in wall paintings, often showing the fruits being picked from cultivated plants. This theme appeared often in Tutankhamun's tomb and in particular on the

cover of an ivory casket where the pharaoh's daughter is shown picking the fruit. Remains of the fruit have not been found in any excavations that have taken place in Egypt, possibly due to its pulpy nature. Experts agree that no remains of plants have been found. P. E. Newberry, who examined the wreathes from Tutankhamun's tomb, identified specimens of mandrake fruits in the floral wreaths on the mummy of Tutankhamun. However, the botanist Nigel F. Hepper examined the actual wreaths many years later and identified the fruit as persea, not mandrake. In some wall scenes the persea fruit is frequently likened to the mandrake fruit, but the persea fruit does not have the prominent calyx that is a feature of the mandrake, and has small reflexed sepals.

In the Syriac medical manuscript published by Sir Ernest Budge, *Syrian Anatomy, Pathology and Therapeutic* (Oxford, 1912, II, 708) a long and interesting passage is devoted to the magical virtues of a plant which can be none other than the mandrake. In this passage it is said: "and after the flower of this fruit... hath died away, there remain on the top thereof two little balls which are like the testicles of the man." There are two kinds of plant, one indigenous (or introduced and acclimatised) in Egypt, and growing in the delta, the other imported from a foreign country. These two species I propose to equate provisionally with *mandragora autumnalis*, of the Mediterranean region, and *mandragora officinarum* which is common in Syrian Palestine. The medicinal uses he lists having studied the papyri from ancient Egypt were for the following external uses: burns, sore tongue, toothache, general pain, and stiff joints. Internally it could be used for pain and contraception.

The above named medicinal uses of the plant called *mstt* are consistent with those to which the mandrake was put by ancient medical writers. The Egyptian papyri states that the fruit is sweet, palatable and mildly astringent.

Mimusops laurifolia (syn. M. schimperi)

Persea
Family: Sopotaceae

A fairly large evergreen tree, growing up to 20 metres high. It was quite commonly cultivated in Egypt during the Pharaonic period but can only be found growing wild in Ethiopia now. The earliest evidence of fruit being used goes back to the Old Kingdom as a result of archaeological discoveries in burial tombs. The leaves of Persea were used in garlands discovered in the tombs of kings in the New Kingdom. Floral garlands found on Rameses II's mummy consisted of persea leaves and petals from lotus flowers, and Tutankhamun's tomb featured two bouquets consisting of olive and persea leaves on a base of common reed. The tree has broad lance-shaped leaves, and near the tips of the branches brown flower buds form later. When the tiny flowers open they are yellow. The fruits then develop and when ripe are yellow and shaped like a Victoria plum approximately 4 cm in length, pointed at the tip. The fruit is sweet with two or three hard seeds, and has pulpy green flesh when eaten. The persea is capable of producing plentiful crops. Theophrastus, the Greek philosopher, sampled the fruit saying how sweet and luscious they were and found them easy to digest even in quantity. Information on the medicinal properties of this tree is lacking, but it was used to treat 'white spots' by using an ointment in which persea fruit is an ingredient.

Moringa peregrina (syn. M. aptera)

Horseradish tree
Family: Moringaceae

The Horseradish tree is deciduous, growing from 10 to 20 metres in height and tending to make slender growth. Its side branches bear small leaflets, which are spaced sparsely. It has small pink flowers in loose panicles during spring, later developing pods up to 30 cm in length, narrow and ribbed, containing three-cornered seeds about 2 cm across. When the seeds are crushed they yield an oil (ben oil) which is yellowish, sweet tasting and odourless. The ancient Egyptians used ben oil for cosmetics, which is frequently mentioned in papyrus texts. Ben oil was also used in cooking. The tree is indigenous to the Jordan valley and as far south as Africa. There is another species *M. pterygosperma* (syn. *M. oleifera*) which produces the same oil but is a native of Sudan. The ancient Egyptians used ben oil medicinally for many ailments but mainly as a carrier for other ingredients. For example, it was combined with honey and sweet beer and used as an enema to ease pain in the anus. Also sore and receding gums were treated by a masticatory composed of ben oil, gum, figs, water, ochre and four unidentified plants. Today it is used internally to treat asthma, gout, rheumatism, enlarged spleen, liver and kidney stones. The oil has anti-bacterial qualities and can be used externally for skin diseases and dental infections.

Moringa prefers a well drained sandy soil in full sun, and is propagated from seed and semi-ripe cuttings. It benefits from annual hard pruning when used for production of leaves, flowers and fruit.

Myrtus communis

Myrtle
Family: Myrtaceae

Myrtle is indigenous in the Mediterranean and North Africa, and is cultivated mainly as a culinary and medicinal herb. This large evergreen shrub can grow up to 3 metres in height and spread, with shiny dark-green lance shaped leaves which when crushed has a similar smell to the juniper. The leaves produce an oil which is used as an ingredient in perfumes. It has fragrant white flowers in spring, later followed by dark blue berries. Myrtle was used by the ancient Egyptians for its medicinal properties, assuming it has been correctly identified in medical papyrus texts. If this is the case then myrtle leaves are used as ingredients in poultices applied externally for swellings (The Hearst  Papyrus, 137), pains (The Ebers Papyrus, 129), stiffness of limbs (Ebers, 672) and removing mucus from the left or right chest (The Berlin Papyrus, 142). It is also a treatment for urinary disorders using ground leaves in fermented plant juice applied externally. Interestingly, today, the medicinal herb is used for urinary infections, dry coughs, bronchial congestion and sinusitis. The oil is still an ingredient in perfumes and to add flavour when cooking pork, lamb and poultry. Leaves of the myrtle and lettuce, ground and added to a mixture of oil, beer and fermented fruit juice, has been boiled and used to treat coughs (Ebers, 312). Dioscorides (1.48) mentions how the fragrant myrtle oil was produced by soaking myrtle leaves in olive oil (presumably the leaves would have to be crushed to release their oil while immersed in olive oil).

To grow satisfactorily this herb requires a sunny position, and soil which is neutral to alkaline and well-drained. It can be reproduced by layering or by seed sown in early spring. Layering is quite easy to achieve and in a few months will produce a good-sized plant. Choose low branches that are more horizontal and flexible enough to be lowered to the soil surface. Make a long slanting cut with a sharp knife halfway through the stem then peg this down into the soil. A covering of soil to a depth of 3 to 5 mm should be enough, and make sure that this area is kept moist to ensure rooting of the stem. Once the branch is firmly rooted it can be detached from the parent plant close to the young rooted plant, which can then be lifted, retaining as much soil as possible, and planted in its permanent position taking care to water sufficiently the first year until fully established.

Nigella sativa

Black Cumin
Family: Ranunculaceae

Black Cumin, also known as nutmeg flower, is an erect growing annual plant 30–40 cm high with finely divided pinnate leaves. White flowers about 3.5 cm across are produced at the ends of the stems, which later develop inflated capsules having horn-like appendages (styles). The capsules contain many black seeds which have a spicy flavour and are used in bread and other cooked foods in India. Seeds and remains of the plant have been discovered in the tomb of Tutankhamun which suggest that the plant grew in Egypt, but it has not been identified in papyrus records. It is useful today for its medicinal properties and is used to improve lactation, stimulate the uterus, for painful menstruation, as a laxative, for haemorrhoids and abscesses. In Egypt, black cumin is propagated by sowing seeds in November. The plants require well drained soil and need to be in full sun.

Nymphaea caerulea and Nymphaea lotus

Blue Lotus and White Lotus
Family: Nymphaeaceae

There are two indigenous species of lotus which were featured in ancient Egyptian art. The blue lotus in particular is a powerful symbol of life and re-birth. These water lilies can be found in Egypt today (although they are quite rare) mainly growing in some of the canals fed by the Nile. The white lotus is known by its Latin name *Nymphaea lotus* and the blue lotus, *Nymphaea caerulea*. The eastern sacred lotus (*Nelumbo nucifera*) was later introduced into Egypt from India. It has pink flowers and round leaves held high above the water surface. The Egyptian lilies have leaves which float on the surface of the water and flower buds held above water level in the early morning before the flowers open. As they open, the flowers float on the surface, and by late afternoon the flowers close and begin to fade, becoming waterlogged and sinking below the water.

The lotus flower featured in ancient Egyptian creation mythology. In the beginning there was the Primordial Ocean called *Nun*. These waters were infinite, covering all distance and direction. Ra rose from the boundless waters (Nun) where he had lived alone in an elemental form. The lotus flower is connected with Ra, who is one of the sun gods, in the sense that the petals close at night and open during the day, representing the sunrise. The Egyptians sometimes symbolised the appearance of the great life spirit out of the waters as a lotus opening its flowers, the petals bending back to reveal the rising god of light and movement. Prior to this nothing else existed — no heaven, no earth, nor any living thing. Sometimes a pharaoh was depicted as representing Ra, and a good example can be found in the form of a beautiful bust from the tomb of Tutankhamun (now in the Cairo Museum) showing him rising from the petals of the lotus as a creating sun god.

The lotus flower is featured in many temples and tombs and in art objects such as jewellery and furniture. The wall paintings in tombs sometimes seemed to show women appearing to sniff the perfume of the blue lotus flower. However, it is not entirely understood why the blue lotus featured so much in Egyptian life and ritual. The flower was obviously appreciated for its beauty and for its scent, which is similar to that of banana. In tomb paintings the lily is shown planted in ponds and lakes of temple and private gardens. Some wall paintings feature revellers wearing cones on their heads made from candle wax, and they may well have included extracts of lotus flowers and myrrh in the ingredients. It is suggested that during the partying the cones would start to melt and trickle down onto their wigs releasing the perfume. The guests also held lotus flowers in their hands — possibly they thought that the scented air would discourage pests and diseases.

The Danish Egyptologist Lise Manniche believes that the lotus flower may have been consumed or sniffed for its narcotic properties. Inscriptions found in the Greco-Roman temple of Horus at Edfu mention the king talking about the virtues of the blue lotus to the god. He says: "When you look at its brilliance your eyes become imbued with dynamic force. When you breathe in your nostrils dilate." (from Joyce Tyldesley, *The Private Lives of the Pharaohs*, *p.*171).

Lise Manniche is not the only person believing that the blue lotus had narcotic characteristics — several other Egyptologists are of the same opinion. With the assistance of a Manchester Museum team of scientists, two researchers, David Counsell and Vic Garner, set out to discover if there were any grounds for this belief. Samples of the blue lotus were obtained from Cairo and Tel Aviv and fresh flowers from a botanical garden in England, grown in conditions resembling those of Egypt. Counsell and Garner suggested that according to the illustrations on tomb and temple walls, the blue lotus could have been incorporated with wine and imbibed or sniffed in order to benefit from its properties. Their tests were unable to show any trace of anything having hallucinogenic properties. However, they discovered that the

samples contained three bioflavonoids known to be beneficial in maintaining and enhancing health. These are natural constituents of fruit, vegetables and flowers and are responsible for their colouring.

It is quite possible that the Egyptians thought the lotus flower had an effect on the libido, as when sniffed or added to wine it prompted emotional craving and specifically human sexual activity.

Olea europaea

Olive
Family: Oleaceae

A slow growing evergreen tree, eventually reaching a height of 9 metres in some cases, preferring a Mediterranean type of climate though it is thought to be a native of Asia Minor. They grow and crop well where they receive winter rains and cool temperatures and hot, dry summers. There is evidence that the olive was cultivated in Egypt at the time of Tutankhamun, and his burial tomb contained wreaths that included olive twigs.

In recent times the olive tree has been cultivated successfully in Egypt but it is necessary to provide irrigation for it to survive in the climate. The yield does not compare favourably with Italian production, unfortunately. Theophrastus, the philosopher, said that it grew in Upper Egypt, and that the oil produced was not inferior to the Greek olive oil he knew, though it had a less pleasing smell. Owing to a gradual change of the climate over the last 2,000 years there would be insufficient rainfall in this area today for it to be worthwhile without irrigation. There is evidence that demand for olives and the oil was so great in the New Kingdom period that they were imported from the area now known as Israel, and from Syria and Greece. Olive trees can live for hundreds of years. They

become gnarled, having grey deeply fissured bark, sometimes becoming hollow, and yet it is suitable for use as timber.

The olive tree has evergreen leaves, which are dark grey-green on the upper surface and lighter green underneath, narrow, lance-shaped and leathery. In cooler climates the trees tend not to flower, yet in Egypt and the Mediterranean numerous white flowers appear in the spring, and later stoned fruits develop. When ripe the black fruits are cold pressed or crushed to produce a fine oil which is valued for its culinary uses and also for its medicinal benefits. As a medicine it is used internally for nervous tension, constipation and peptic ulcers. The oil has some useful properties if consumed with food on a regular basis; it lowers blood pressure, thus reducing the risk of circulatory disease. It is also used externally for softening the skin. Despite its medicinal benefits, there is no evidence of it being used for this purpose in ancient Egypt. The ancient Egyptians used olive oil to fuel their lamps, and as a carrier oil in which to immerse fragrant scented flowers. It may also be consumed with food.

The olive can be propagated from seed sown in autumn or by semi-ripe cuttings taken in summer.

Origanum syriacum

Marjoram, Origanum, Sweet marjoram, Bible hyssop, Syrian oregano
Family: Labiatae

Origanum syriacum is a low perennial shrub, which has medicinal and culinary uses. This species is native to middle eastern areas which includes the Sinai Peninsula and Mediterranean coastal regions. It grows up to 90 cm in height making a bushy plant with mainly erect stems. It has egg-shaped leaves (ovate) varying in size depending on whether it is growing in areas shaded by rocks or in full sun, where the leaves are larger. Flower spikes of dense tiny flowers are on the ends of main stems, and many lateral side branches, forming a pyramid of lilac flowers (a branched raceme).

The plant is in danger of being over-exploited, leading to its gradual disappearance in its natural habitats. It has become rare in the rocky mountain areas of Sinai. It will grow in dry to moist light sandy to loamy medium soils which are well drained. The plants growing in Sinai appear to be a variant or subspecies of *O. syriacum* named *Origanum maru* variety sinaicum, which is also indigenous to Egypt and the Middle East. To protect the plant in its natural habitats some areas have been fenced off to prevent grazing by animals.

For medicinal use the plants are cut down when the flowers are beginning to fade. The dried leaves are mainly used, though dried leaves and flowers are used for seasoning in cooking. The dried parts of the plant are packed in large sacks of jute and stored on slatted wood staging allowing free movement of air. The storage shed must be dry and well ventilated to prevent dampness and fungal damage, and rodents and insects must be kept away. Beneficial oil obtained from the leaf of the plant is antiseptic, and is good for skin health. It is also used as a scent in soaps and lotions. The herb is much appreciated for its medicinal properties in the modern world of today and has a long history of use. An infusion obtained by boiling the dried leaves and flowers in

water is said to be beneficial for the relief of coughs and colds, bronchitis, indigestion and tooth decay. It's value as a drug has been tested by laboratory experiments which analysed the chemical constituents of extracted essential oils and fresh and dried parts of the plant, and claim that it is an effective natural antioxidant and capable of preventing fungal, microbial, and parasitic activity.

Origanum has for a long time been recognised for its use as a herb for seasoning meats and vegetables. In the Middle East and Mediterranean areas its dried leaves are mixed with sumach, sesame seed and other herbs and known as Za'atar. In these areas it is commonly sprinkled on bread with olive oil or added to the surface of bread dough and then baked. The leaves and dried flower heads gathered before losing their colour have almost the same flavour as a combination of thyme, oregano and marjoram. The finely powdered dry flowers on their own enhance the taste of tomato soup and cooked cheese giving them a distinctive flavour.

Origanum is easily cultivated to allow an increase in available material for use in pharmaceutical and herbal preparations. Stocks of plants can be increased by propagating from seed, division and cuttings. Seeds can be sown outdoors into prepared ground either in the spring or autumn, or sown in February to March in a greenhouse. Alternatively, plants that have been established for three years or more can easily be divided by lifting a clump of plants and splitting with the aid of a fork and a sharp spade or a large sharp knife. This task is best carried out in March or October. Basal cuttings can be taken in June when new shoots are emerging around the established plants. Ideal shoots are best when about 10 cm above the ground, severed from the parent plant with as much underground stem as possible. When the young plants are established place them in a lightly shaded cold frame and allow to become well established before planting out later in the summer.

Papaver rhoeas

Corn Poppy or Field Poppy
Family: Papaveraceae

This poppy grew in the first world war on the battlefields of Flanders after the ground had been disturbed by shelling, which enabled the seeds to germinate. The seeds can remain dormant for many years and only emerge because of the disturbance to the ground. Also the red poppy flowers were often seen in corn fields before the grain crop was harvested. The poppy develops seed capsules that are likened to a pepper pot — when the wind blows it acts as a shaker scattering the ripe seeds. Sometimes the dispersal of these seeds tended to occur when the grain was being harvested and it is suggested by some experts that by this means poppy seeds spread into many countries. This poppy is thought to be a native of the eastern Mediterranean countries. It certainly grew in Egypt, judging by a casket found in the tomb of Tutankhamun which featured this poppy on the lid and the stick bouquets produced for funerals of many pharaohs. This annual poppy has scarlet flowers about 5 to 8 cm across with four petals usually with a blue-black blotch at the base and purple stamens. It makes a plant about 20–60 cm in height having pinnate leaves covered in long hairs that clasp the stem. All parts of the plant, when cut or bruised, produce a white latex which is toxic, with the exception of the seeds that can be used for culinary purposes. The dark brown seeds are added to breads, pastries and meat dishes, and to cooked foods for decorative effect. Medicinally it is used as a sedative for coughs and digestive problems.

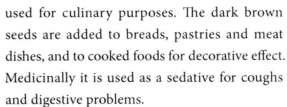

136

Papaver somniferum

Common Poppy or Opium Poppy
Family: Papaveraceae

This annual plant has wavy irregular pinnate greyish-green leaves, and fairly erect growth, and grows to a height variable up to 1.5 metres. It produces flowers which are usually pink but sometimes white, having four wavy petals about 10 to 16 cm in diameter with yellow anthers and stamens. Later a capsule develops which contains a large number of grey seeds which are dispersed in the same way as the field poppy through pores when shaken by wind. This poppy is cultivated for the drug opium, known to be used in ancient Egypt, and first recorded by the Sumerians during the fourth millennium BC. Prospero Alpini described the effect it had on the Egyptian people, saying it had a stimulating effect encouraging men in war and in love and likely to cause psychedelic dreams. Its cultivation and use is now subject to legal restrictions and can only be grown for medicinal purposes. This herb is a source for the illicit drug heroin and the latex in the plant contains morphine used medicinally to treat severe pain. Like the field poppy it is safe to use the seeds in cooking or as a garnish.

Phoenix dactylifera

Date Palm
Family: Palmae

The Latin or scientific name *Phoenix* is thought to have been derived by the ancient Greeks and referred to the tree itself. It is said to have been found on the Mediterranean coast in what is now Israel and South Lebanon, called Phoenicia at the time by the famous botanist Theophrastus (370–285 BC). The ancient Greeks also gave the name Phoenix to a legendary bird which caused fear in the hearts of men and women alike. Predating this period of history the ancient Egyptians also mentioned the legendary Bennu bird which resembled the grey heron commonly found in the Nile valley or Goliath heron from the coast of the red sea.

They attached such great importance to this bird, which became symbolically connected to the sun and was considered to be the soul of the Sun God, Ra. In an elaborated stylistic form it featured in mural paintings in the tombs of the Pharaohs and important officials. The Egyptians revered the date as highly as the sun-bird, and the term 'Bennu' also applied to it and all things that taste sweet.

The fleshy parts of date palm fruits were discovered in a beer cocktail contained in a vat at an excavation site in Hierakonpolis, dating back to 3450 BC. Since Pharaonic times the date palm has been cultivated in the Middle East and dry sub-tropical regions. The plant was probably developed some time before the Pre-dynastic period by selecting from wild forms growing in the area. Vegetative propagation seems to have been the main method of increasing stocks and is achieved by taking suckers from the base of mature palms. Soil is heaped up around the base of the plant to encourage the formation of roots and once a good root system has become established, the new plant can be detached from its parent and transplanted into a nursery bed.

The date palm is tolerant of high levels of salinity and can withstand being irrigated with brackish water where fresh water is not available in desert or coastal areas. When the Pharaohs were in power in Egypt and up to the time when the Aswan Dam was built, the land in the Nile Valley was inundated every year. As the palm tree was often grown near the banks of the Nile it was quite possible for them to be flooded for several weeks without receiving any

139

damage. In ideal conditions the trunk can exceed 15 metres in height with leaves up to 6 metres in length. The leaves are pinnate, like a very large feather in shape, with leaflets arising from opposite sides of a common axis or midrib.

The date palm needs to be pollinated to produce fruits, and for this to be most reliably achieved it is necessary to have both male and female trees near to each other. The proportion of female trees to males can be quite large providing enough pollen from the male trees is obtained to pollinate all the female trees in a plantation. This could not be done except by artificial means; it is likely that the trees would have been climbed by agile young farm or garden labourers and hand pollinated. Having successfully achieved cross pollination, large clusters of fruit developed and were gathered when ripe.

The fruit was highly regarded and eaten as an essential part of the Egyptian diet. Dates can be eaten fresh, although they were normally pressed into blocks after drying in direct sun for two to three days and could be stored for long periods for eating when required. For ease of handling in this pressed form, the blocks were threaded onto strings, and even in modern times compressed dates can still be purchased. According to Lise Manniche, the labourers at Dier el-Medina received compressed dates in part payment of wages, as well as other basic foods and beer. The juice obtained due to compressing the fresh fruits was often combined with honey to sweeten beer and foods because in those days cane and beet sugars were unknown, and it is used as a base medium in medicines.

The Egyptians made wine from dates by soaking the fresh fruit in water and later squeezing the liquid from the pulp which was then fermented. Though detrimental to the tree, some of the estate farmers tapped the palm trees for their sap and the liquid was fermented to produce a liqueur. However, if this was done too often, or too much sap was taken at one time, the plant would die. The leaves of the tree were manufactured into woven mats, brushes, thread, ropes, boat rigging and sandals, and timber for roofing was provided by the trunk.

The date seed or stone is very hard, long, narrow and grooved along its entire length, and many well preserved seeds have been found during excavations of tombs. According to Dr Wafaa M. Amer, diggings carried out at the Abusir tombs in Giza unearthed date seeds which were included in mortuary offerings (*c.*2950 BC). Seeds were also found in the tomb of Tutankhamun, though it is likely that fresh dates were offered, but that they rotted leaving the hard seed only.

The date palm often featured in tomb paintings depicting the gardens of important officials. The walled gardens featured date palms and other trees providing shade around a pool in the centre, such as in the tomb of Nebamun, an 18th Dynasty official. The capitals of stone columns sometimes feature palm leaves carved in relief, like those remaining in Abusir carved with the name of King Sahure, and those found at Philae, which also feature bunches of dates. Hathor, the goddess of life, joyfulness, music, dancing, inebriety and fertility, had the date palm as one of her emblems.

Pluchea dioscoridis

Ploughman's Spikenard or Marsh Fleabane
Family: Compositae

Pluchea dioscoridis is a shrub, widespread in Africa and Arabian countries including Egypt, and commonly found in the Nile Valley and the Delta region. To grow successfully it prefers moist, fine loamy soils, and to be near water courses such as irrigation channels, drains, streams and tributaries of the Nile. Its height can vary from one to three metres, making a bushy many branched shrub, with cylindrical stems that are slightly hairy. The leaves are alternately arranged, attached directly to the stems, and ovate with serrated edges and stipules at the leaf base. The flowers are close together, arranged in clusters, often attached by short stems. Sometimes several clusters form a loose rounded head of flowers. The florets around the outer edge of each cluster are pistillate (female) while the few central flowers are hermaphrodite. When in bud the flowers are cream, turning pink as they open, and later forming small, smooth, ribbed fruits containing one seed.

Although the plant is regarded as an invasive weed it is valued for its medicinal properties, and modern chemical analysis has shown that it could be useful in a number of other ways. A tea of fresh leaves infused in boiling water and sieved is drunk in Egypt to treat colds and for calming the digestive system. In North America the oil extracted from this plant is used as an ingredient in a hair care product which includes peppermint and rosemary as a conditioner and detangler. Scientific tests have shown that extracts of *Pluchea dioscoridis* can be successfully used as an insecticide against harvested grain pests when in dry storage silos or sheds. The earlier name for this plant is *Conyza dioscoridis*, which is derived from 'konis', meaning 'dust', as the powdered leaves when sprinkled were considered capable of keeping flies away.

Punica granatum

Pomegranate
Family: Lythraceae

Punica granatum is a large shrub or small tree that grows to between two and four metres in height. It is mainly cultivated in Mediterranean countries and was introduced to Egypt during the 18th Dynasty. It usually makes a many branched bush having numerous spines, and small narrow leathery leaves which are absent during winter. The new foliage in spring tends to be coppery in colour, turning golden in the autumn before dropping. The attractive flowers appear at the height of summer; they are quite large and bright orange-red followed by a fruit having a hard leathery skin with a prominent calyx. The fruit is about the size of an apple and when ripe is coppery yellow, tinged pink and purple. It is filled with many seeds surrounded by a juicy pulp having a pleasant taste and quite refreshing.

During one of his campaigns, Tuthmosis III brought back living trees of pomegranate from Western Asia. The pomegranate tree was featured in Inenis' garden at Thebes along with other trees, and one is depicted on the wall of a Theban tomb (No.217) bearing flowers. The dried remains of a pomegranate fruit was found in the tomb of Dyehuyu (Queen Hatshepsut's butler) along with other offerings.

The ancient Egyptians ate the fruit, and they used the juice from it to produce wine. In present day Egypt its juice is used as a drink. The rind combined with water makes a yellow dye used for dyeing leather, and in some middle eastern countries still serves the same purpose. Apart from this it was useful for its medicinal properties. For instance, the root can be ground into a pulp with water and strained to take as a drink for the elimination of tapeworm or even roundworm. It is also said to be beneficial for stomach complaints using the root crushed in beer, which is left to stand overnight and then strained. Water is then added to the remaining liquid in the proportions of three to one, and taken as a drink.

Ricinus communis

Castor-oil Plant
Family: Euphorbiaceae

An evergreen shrub found growing wild in the Middle East and Africa including Egypt where it grows by the Nile. It has soft stemmed bushy growth with large palmate toothed leaves, growing up to 60 cm long where water is plentiful, usually green and having dark red stems. It produces green flowers without petals in summer, and fruits later form which are prickly and globular, containing three seeds. The seeds are poisonous, capable of causing death to humans and animals, although castor-oil has beneficial medicinal properties. The oil from the crushed seeds was used for lighting lamps and cosmetics in ancient Egypt. The plant is still widely grown commercially, particularly for the oil which is used by manufacturers of soaps, lubricating oils, candles, cosmetics and so on. In Pharaonic times workers who were involved in building the pyramids and based at Deir el Medina were said to be given castor-oil as part of their wages. It is thought that the oil was for anointing the body, possibly for lamp oil, and as an emollient for the skin.

Castor oil was commonly used in cases of constipation or infection to clear the bowel, and is described as a purgative.

Sesamum indicum

Sesame
Family: Pedaliaceae

An annual plant up to 1 metre in height, tending to be branched with a spread of at least 45 cm, the stems clothed in fine hairs. It tends to have a strong smell when the leaves are squeezed or when brushed against. The leaves near the base are large and divided; higher up the stem they become smaller, more narrow and lance-shaped, deeply veined. Sesamum produces white or pink bell-shaped flowers in a loose cluster or spike in the summer, later developing seed pods which contain creamy white oily seeds.

This species in indigenous in tropical Africa and Asia and in the present day is grown as a crop in those areas for the seeds. There is no record of the plants being grown in ancient Egypt, but it is known that the Egyptians used sesame oil at least from the 18th Dynasty onwards. Dioscorides mentions that the Egyptians used Sesame oil made from the seeds and said it was good for eye problems when combined with wine (I.121). The ancient Egyptians used the oil in medicines, perfumes, lamps and also ate the seeds. It is possible that the people of those days used the seeds in the same way as they do now in the Middle East, sprinkled on bread before baking. Seeds are ground into a paste to use as a spread on bread (tahini) and combined with honey to eat as a confection (halva). Sesame seeds are highly nutritious and calorific containing appreciable levels of vitamins A, B and E and Calcium salts, and the oil is unsaturated. Adding the seeds to food is useful in that they strengthen bones and teeth and as a tonic that improves kidney and liver function. The other medicinal benefits claimed for sesame are quite wide; for

example, it is administered to patients with osteoporosis, dry cough, tinnitus, poor sight, and also used as a mild laxative.

The plants can be propagated by seed, preferring well-drained sandy soil. Seeds can be sown outdoors directly into their permanent quarters in early February protected by cloches or polythene. Once the seeds have germinated and the seedlings have started to grow they can be thinned out gradually until the plants are 38–45 cm apart. Also, once the seedlings are growing well the polythene can be removed during the day, and gradually removed entirely by April. While the plants are protected they need watering, preferably in the evenings or very early morning to avoid the leaves being scorched by hot sun.

Solanum nigrum

Black nightshade and Hound's berry
Family: Solonaceae

Also the varieties *incisum* and *elbaensis*. This plant is related to the tomato and is similar in shape, though the fruits are smaller. It is an annual species which is very adaptable and widespread around the world, withstanding a wide range of conditions from temperate to tropical, and low to high altitudes to at least 3,500 metres. Typically, as a common weed, it is capable of flowering at an early stage well before maturity in difficult conditions, and seeding prolifically. Frequently found growing on road-side verges, next to hedgerows, at the edges of cultivated arable land, wasteland and other habitats. Will tolerate dry soils and quite extreme temperature during Egyptian summers.

In ideal conditions this annual plant will reach a height of 70 cm. It is erect in habit, rather similar to the domesticated tomato, except in miniature. Also, foliage and stems are similar in colour, side growths emerge from the leaf axils in the same way, and the flower stems emerge from the main stem in a similar way. The stems tend to be covered in fine hairs like the leaves though sometimes they can be quite smooth and glossy. The leaves can be up to 7 cm in length by 3.5 cm in width, varying in shape from lanceolate to ovate and usually entire though sometimes can be indented. The variety *incisum* has deeply incised and dentate leaves very similar to the tomato leaf in shape and tex-ture, though much smaller. The flowers are attached to a short stem, up to ten in a cluster and five petalled. The flowers are white, and later small green berries start to form which when ripe are round, shiny and black up to 1 cm in diameter. Although *Solanum nigrum* is indigenous

in Egypt, particularly in the Nile valley, in several oases including the Fayum and in all the Egyptian deserts, there is no record of how it was used in ancient times. Evidence from other countries shows that in the past it was valued for its medicinal properties and recent research shows it can be beneficial in many ways.

The whole plant is pulled out of the ground when most of the fruits have ripened, and is allowed to dry in the sun and then stored for use as a herb. The plant is also used fresh as a traditional folk medicine and all parts are used for various ailments, some quite serious. In some countries it is used as a food source for humans as well as useful fodder and browsing for cattle, goats and sheep, yet many species of Solanum are said to be poisonous including *Solanum nigrum,* which is listed in early texts throughout the world as being toxic and a cause of death in humans and livestock. However there is evidence to show that the plant can be used as a vegetable where the leaves and young shoots are boiled in water. The vegetable is quite nutritious, providing proteins, Vitamins A and C, and minerals typically found in other green vegetables such as calcium, phosphorous and iron. It is used in soups and sauces and for cooking as a vegetable in Africa, Asia, Malaysia and the Americas, and in Australia as a fairly recent introduction. Native tribes in Kenya used boiled leaves for pregnant women believing that eating this vegetable assisted recuperation after delivery. If the berries are picked whilst still green they need to be cooked. It is widely accepted that the fruits can be eaten when they are ripe usually when black, although some variants of the species can also be red or yellow. The fruit, like the leaves, have beneficial characteristics as a food and contain calcium, iron, carotene and Vitamins B and C. The berries are used in pies, jams and preserves, and also as a dye and a food colourant. According to Fortuin and Omta who did research in Java, *Solanum nigrum* has several characteristics that by cross breeding or hybridization could be bred into useful commercial crops. For example, resistance to tobacco mosaic virus, potato late blight, Phomopsis fruit rot and atrazine resistance are characteristics worthy of incorporation.

149

Therapeutically, parts of the plant used on their own are said to be valuable for treating many disorders. For instance, the juice from the crushed leaves is said to be effective for chronic enlargement of the liver and cirrhosis of the liver, and is also able to relieve painful menstruation. Toxicity of the liver and kidneys caused by drugs and chemicals can be reduced by a decoction of its leaves, and it is capable of improving the health of these vital organs. Boiled leaves may be mashed to form a paste and used as a poultice, applied externally to the skin or to affected areas for psoriasis, ringworm and swellings caused, for example, by bruising. A decoction of berries and flowers is recommended for coughs and colds, and berries on their own for fevers, eye diseases and hydrophobia. A decoction of leaves is also said to be effective as an antiseptic and diuretic. All parts of the plants are beneficial as an emollient or as a laxative. *Solanum nigrum* is used as an ingredient in several pharmaceutical preparations or herbal medicines, for diseases and conditions such as dysentery, hepatitis, insomnia, sclerosis of the arteries and other circulatory disorders, and for improving assimilation of foods.

The plant is easily reproduced by seeds usually spread by birds eating the ripe berries. For cultivation the seeds can be extracted from the fruits when over ripe.

Solenostemma arghel

Argel or Arghel
Family: Asclepiadaceae

The Arghel is found in desert regions, particularly in the Sahara, Sinai and the Southern Eastern Desert, which includes Egypt. It is a small perennial shrub growing up to one metre in height, mainly evergreen throughout its life although some plants in long dry periods shed all their leaves. The useful life-span is not much more than three years, and it normally produces most of its flowers at the end of this time to ensure reproduction of the species. It grows mainly in gravely or pebbly soils and it can be found in Wadi Umm Hargel, from which it takes its name according to K. H. Batanouny in the *Encyclopedia of Wild Medicinal Plants in Egypt.*

The many branched shrub has erect stems covered in fine soft downy hairs which are adpressed but smooth in texture and blue-green. The leaves are greyish-green to yellowish-green, lanceolate and quite downy like the stems, and about 2 to 4 cm in length with pointed apex. The leaf margins tend to be rolled inwards and the simply shaped leaves are attached opposite to each other, tending to be thick and rigid. The leaves and stems of the plant are covered in dense minute hairs and enable it to adapt to drought conditions, reducing loss of moisture through transpiration. Towards the growing tips of the branches flowers are formed in the leaf axils which are white and numerous in a compact umbel-like head, though a little more rounded in shape. The normal flowering period can be any time from September to April. Later, fruits are formed which are coloured pale pink-beige streaked purple, ovate in shape and about 5 cm long. The almost pointed end of the fruit hangs downwards and has a tuft of hairs emerging from the tip. The hard skinned outer-shell of the fruit eventually dries out, breaking open to reveal many ovoid seeds each with a tuft of hairs attached allowing the seeds to float in the air and disperse.

151

In Egypt there is great demand for this plant to the extent that collection from the wild is threatening its existence. Because it is so important as a medicinal plant, trials are being carried out to decide how it can be propagated and cultivated in order to increase stocks commercially and protect it from extinction in the wild habitats. Experiments have shown that seeds sown in sandy soil germinate and make the best plants producing the most seeds. The percentage of germination both in the soil and in the laboratory was highest with a temperature of 35 °C. Leaves of the plant are best collected after fruiting between April and June when chemical content is highest, although they are collected throughout the year. Usually stems of the Arghel are gathered together in small bunches and hung in warm buildings, well ventilated and dark for drying. When dry the leaves are separated from the stems and stored in sterile dark glass jars with screw top lids. Today its value as a recognised contemporary Egyptian folk medicine is certainly known according to K. H. Batanouny, who claims it is used as a purgative, antipyretic, expectorant and antispasmodic. Also it is used to treat neuralgia, sciatica and in the form of leaf infusions for gastro-intestinal cramps, colic, colds and urinary tract problems.

Tamarix aphylla (syn. T. articulata)

Tamarisk
Family: Tamaricaceae

A native species to Egypt which is capable of tolerating salt spray and even soils or sands affected by salt in coastal areas such as the Delta. It can be found growing by river or canal banks, in dry river beds which rarely flood, and can survive long periods without water. Tamarix when mature makes a large shrub or tree which produces very deep roots to find water in sandy soils. When the Suez Canal was being constructed, it is reputed that Tamarix roots reached to a depth of 50 metres. It is

153

often used as a windbreak. Its large trunk is suitable for timber, and was used in ancient Egypt for construction work owing to its density and strength. There are other Tamarix species native to Egypt, one of them being *Tamarix nilotica*. The species are similar, varying in leaf colour, which is mainly greyish-green or green-shaded blue-grey. The leaves are densely arranged on close twiggy growth and are like tiny needles; if looked at from a few metres away the foliage has a feathery appearance. The tree is able to survive long dry periods, partly due to the leaves having evolved in such a way as to reduce water loss to a minimum. Also, it is quite common to have secretions of salt on the leaves in a maritime situation. The flowers are either pink or white, appearing towards the ends of the branches in spikes or racemes, and the individual flowers are without petals. 'Fruits' form shortly after flowering which are capsules containing several seeds.

Some historical texts suggest that the 'fruit' referred to was a sweet deposit which forms on the branches as a result of insects extracting juice or resin from the tree which looks like a gall. This is thought to be the substance that the Israelites collected in the desert called Manna (Exodus 16). The 'fruit' was suitable as an infusion to treat the eyes according to Dioscorides (1.118). Today the Egyptians use the fruit as a herbal medicine for haemorrhages, dysentery and the eyes.

Teucrium polium

Mountain germander, Cat Thyme and Hulwort
Family: Labiatae

Teucrium polium is a variable species which seems able to adapt to difficult conditions and will grow in moist or dry soil often in stony ground, preferring neutral to alkaline soil. This perennial plant requires full sun and is mainly found growing in sandy situations in mountainous regions and lower altitudes down to coastal areas and desert. It makes a many branched bushy plant up to 40 cm high in suitable conditions when in flower. The plant has a woody base up to 14 cm before branching, with the many stems being greyish green to white, densely covered with very fine woolly hairs which reduce water loss in hot arid conditions. It is also capable of growing in rich loamy soils and even heavy clay soils if well drained. Due to variations in habitat there are some subspecies and isolated plant colonies which have adapted to their own situations. Some can be sparse in their growth due to very dry conditions, or bushy where in more moist areas or micro-climates. The leaves are attached directly to the branches and are ovate to linear in shape, with notched edges, 1 to 3 cm in length, and greyish-green. Flowers appear from April to August, in white dense globose heads, scented and bisexual, pollinated by bees. After self-fertilisation the brown seeds become ripe from July to August. The plant is distributed in the Mediterranean region, in the coastal areas of Egypt to the Libyan border, and Sinai peninsula. It can also be found in Arabia, Iran, Iraq, Somalia, Southern Russia, Balkans and Afghanistan.

The plant is often dried after flowering and stored in a dry ventilated place until required for use in medicines. It can be propagated by cuttings or seeds. Ideally the seed is sown in trays of compost containing at least 50 percent gritty sand in the spring in a cold frame. Once the seeds have germinated the seedlings are pricked off singly into small pots when large enough to handle and later planted into permanent ground.

Teucrium polium has been traditionally used as a herbal drug to expel worms by infusing the dried plant in hot water and allowing to cool sufficiently for drinking after straining. Young tender shoots and leaves infused in boiling water are used as a stimulant and purifier, as a tea sweetened with sugar, for stomach upsets, and intestinal problems, but only using young tender shoots and leaves. Powdered leaf extract is known to substantially increase insulin secretion, and therefore is beneficial for diabetes sufferers.

Thymus spicata

Wild Thyme
Family: Labiatae

The Thymes mainly come from southern Europe, the Mediterranean and Asia, although *T. spicata* is mainly found growing in the eastern Mediterranean but no further south than Israel. This suggests that it did not grow in Egypt, yet remains of *Thymus spicata* were found in Tutankhamun's tomb. However, it was not unusual for herbs and spices in a dried state to be traded by other Middle Eastern countries.

Like most thymes it is a woody perennial which is a bushy, many stemmed evergreen plant growing up to 30 cm high. The leaves are attached to the stems in pairs, 1 to 2 cm in length, looking very similar to the common thyme (*T. vulgaris*) though fewer in number. The flowers are formed from five sepals fused together to form a two-lipped tube, the lower lip being three lobed and purplish in colour. Small flowers are produced in clusters or short spikes towards the ends of the stems. The leaves of all thymes are aromatic and produce a rich volatile oil which is mainly thymol, useful as an antiseptic in toothpastes. The main species used today for medicinal purposes are *T. serpyllum* and *T. vulgaris*, but there is no information as to what use the ancient Egyptians made of *T. spicata* or any other species. It is known that thyme is grown in Egypt today, particularly *T. vulgaris* which is an ingredient in bouquet garni and to flavour casseroles, soups and stuffings. The latter species is used medicinally to treat coughs, bronchitis, and other throat complaints, gum disease and indigestion. Thymes prefer well-drained soils, although *T. spicata* will grow in drier stony soils, and all species need a sunny position. All the species propagate from seed sown in spring or stocks of plants increased by softwood or semi-hardwood cuttings taken in the summer.

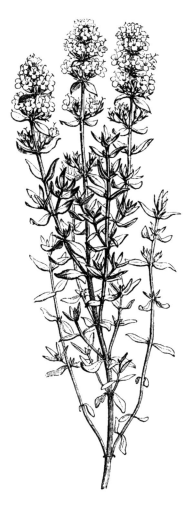

Trigonella foenum-graecum

Fenugreek
Family: Leguminosae

Fenugreek is a native of the Mediterranean region, the Middle East and India and its cultivation in Egypt goes back to about 3000 BC based on remains found. It is an annual plant grown for fodder in Egypt and for human consumption as a vegetable using the leaves or the young shoots for salad. The seeds are ground to use as one of the spices in curry powder, which is mainly used in Indian cooking, while the seeds are included in stews and bread in Egypt. Fenugreek is an aromatic plant which has trifoliate leaves, producing one to two usually white flowers in the leaf axils in March and April. Narrow beak-like pods develop later containing several yellowish brown seeds which have a high protein content. In ancient Egypt the plant was valued for its medicinal properties, particularly to aid child birth and encourage weight gain

after illness and for under-nourished poor people. Today it is used for digestive disorders, to improve lactation, painful menstruation, labour pains and tuberculosis. Fenugreek prefers to have full sun and a well drained fertile soil, and is propagated from seeds.

Triticum dicoccum

Emmer Wheat
Family: Gramineae

This particular species of annual grass has long been superseded by higher yielding wheats. It goes back to ancient times; no-one knows its origins but it was grown in Egypt possibly before 5000 BC. It was used as a bread wheat up to the time when the Romans took possession of Egypt and they introduced a higher yielding species, perhaps *Triticum aestivum*; this species and hybrid varieties of it are now commonly grown for wheat flour.

Emmer wheat had seven ears on one stem, each ear bearing whiskery hair-like appendages which are attached to the grains. The idea that this wheat had seven ears may be a myth derived from the allegory or bible story mentioned in Genesis 41.5–7: "And it came to pass at the end of two years, that Pharaoh dreamed: and behold, he stood by the river ... And he slept and dreamed the second time: and behold seven ears of corn came up upon one stalk, rank and good. And behold seven thin ears, blasted with the east wind, sprung up after them. And the seven thin ears devoured the seven rank and full ears. And Pharaoh awoke, and behold, it was a dream." According to Joseph who interpreted the Pharaohs dreams it meant seven years of plenty and seven years of famine.

In Italy, emmer wheat is grown on high altitude land, as it crops successfully under these conditions.

The growth is typical for a tall grass producing several narrow green leaves eventually terminating in a green whiskery flower head. The flower later develops a broad head consisting of four to six rows of seeds or grains which expand, and as they ripen the remaining part of the plant turns golden yellow.

The harvesting of the grain in Pharaonic times was quite a laborious process usually taking place in June. Labourers first cut the heads

from the stems with a sickle and gathered them from the ground into baskets, which were carried to a level piece of ground for threshing. Threshing (removing the grains from the ear) was achieved by dragging a heavy wooden sledge drawn by men or animals many times around the threshing floor or hitting the ears with a flail. The final part of the process, known as winnowing, removed the chaff from the grain. The grains were scooped up and tossed into the air allowing the light chaff to blow away leaving the grains to fall to the floor. The grain could then be scooped up into sacks ready to be carried to the granary for dry storage. Assuming the threshing ground was stone paved and brushed clean they may not have sieved the grains before filling the sacks. Grain was the main staple of the ancient Egyptian diet and was used as a means of barter for goods that workers may need to purchase. The evidence from papyrus is that grain was also given to workers as pay.

During the period when the Romans ruled Egypt, the Fayum region was the major provider of wheat grain for the Roman Empire (Britain was the second most important producer under Roman rule).

Osiris was the god of agriculture and also the god of corn (his death being associated with the reaping of the grain). The mythology suggests that Osiris showed the Egyptians how to cultivate the land and produce suitable tools to achieve this. The Pharaohs liked to be regarded as the gods on earth, or the sons of god in waiting, performing the tasks of the various gods that the people worshipped. With regard to Osiris, the Pharaohs had their tombs decorated to illustrate them ploughing the fields. In the tomb of Sennedjem (a regional representative to the King) at Deir el Medina, Thebes, he and his wife are shown reaping the corn. In the British Museum a painted wooden figure of Osiris wearing a white crown and holding a crook and flail, a royal insignia adorned with two plumes, is displayed. Most of his body is dotted with seeds of corn arranged in circles, each circle containing nine seeds spaced in an even pattern.

Every year at the time of planting the seed, the people knelt down and prayed for the crop to flourish, and ultimately for a successful harvest.

They made hollowed out symbolic wooden seed trays in the shape of his figure filled with dark moist Nile mud or soil. If the seeds produced green shoots then it was thought that there would be a good crop to follow. An Osiris seed tray was found in the tomb of Tutankhamun containing grain that had actually sprouted, signifying the mythical rebirth of the dead pharaoh. The moist soil would have ensured the germination of the seeds. Because of the dry warm atmosphere of the tomb, the embryonic roots and shoots were preserved sufficiently to be recognizable, and any further growth was curtailed by lack of sunlight. It was believed that Osiris had the earth within his possession and could control the growth of any plant emerging from the earth. The King was also thought to have the same divine powers of Osiris and it was considered that the earth that he trod would be blessed. The gathering in of the grain harvest was a time to celebrate, assuming the crop was good.

Vicia faba

Broad Bean
Family: Leguminosae

The Broad Bean has been grown in Egypt since early Pharaonic times and is frequently found with burial remains. It was common to use beans as a means of counting votes from the people, for example to elect an important official. Each person would select from two beans, a black one meant a 'no' vote and green signified a 'yes' vote. It is grown as an annual, reaching a height of 1 metre with thick erect stems, having grey-green leaves that are lighter green underneath. Later, white pea-like flowers are produced which have a black blotch on the upright petals and are usually scented. In Egypt the bean seeds are sown in December into fertile prepared soil which is capable of being irrigated when needed. By late February the flowers are produced, which later result in a crop of bean pods containing three to six seeds ready for harvesting in late June. Egyptians regard boiled beans as part of their staple diet and they are to be found incorporated into some wheat breads. This bean does not appear to have any medicinal value.

Vitis vinifera

Grape Vine
Family: Vitaceae

The grape vine is a deciduous climbing shrub which over several years develops a woody stem bearing many long sappy green shoots during the growing season. In the winter, cultivated grape vines are dormant, and while they are in this state all the side shoots are pruned hard back to the stem. When the warmer weather comes in spring, leaf buds start to swell very soon producing rapidly growing shoots, each one usually bearing five to seven palmate leaves when fully developed and having several appendages (tendrils) towards the end of the shoots enabling them to cling to a wooden frame or pergola. The leaves are normally arranged alternately with small clusters of flowers carried opposite one of the leaves and often half way along each shoot.

The cultivated form of grape is self-fertile, unlike wild ones which will only develop fruit if male and female plants are close enough to each other to allow pollination. Once fertilisation has taken place the small green fruits begin to swell, eventually becoming ripe towards the end of summer. At this stage the fruit is juicy and sweet enough to eat, although the swelling grapes in the bunches have to be thinned out to obtain large fruits for eating purposes. Depending on the variety the ripe fruits are either green, red or black and can be used for eating, wine making or dried in the sun to produce raisins.

Cultivation of the vine in ancient

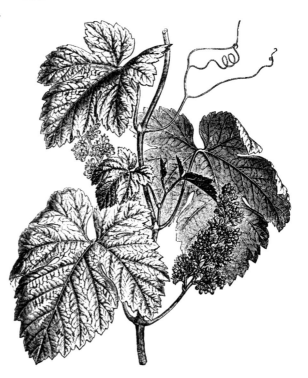

163

Egypt goes back to the fourth millennium BC with vineyards being most prominent in the Nile delta and also in the oases, particularly the Fayum and Dakhlah. The grape vines used for production of wine and fruit for eating in ancient Egypt was a cultivated form as far as can be ascertained. The vines and grapes illustrated on walls in private tombs appear to show fruit of a sufficient size to suggest cultivated vines were grown. An imitation bunch of black grapes which was found in a sealed tomb can now be seen in a display cabinet in the Cairo Agricultural Museum; this could also be included as evidence of grapes being grown in ancient Egypt. The wild form would not produce grapes of sufficient size to be suitable for eating, particularly considering the number of seeds within the small fruit.

Included in the finds of Tutankhamun's tomb were baskets containing several types of fruit used as offerings, and shrivelled grapes were identified. It is quite common for grape pips to

Artificial grapes as displayed in the Egyptian Agriculture Museum.

be found in excavated Egyptian tombs and buildings as they are very hard and don't decay in such dry conditions. High priests and successive Pharaohs used wine in their offering rituals for the gods on a regular basis, probably daily. Also, the Pharaoh, his relatives, and privileged guests, drank wine at their banquets, and this is frequently depicted in wall paintings. The processes of vine growing and wine-making were also illustrated in private tombs from 2575 BC onwards. They show the

grapes being picked by hand and then carried in baskets to the place where grapes are pressed by men treading the fruit with their feet in what appear to be stone troughs.

Presumably the crushed grapes and the juice was then scooped up and placed in clay jars to allow the process of fermentation to take place. When fermentation was completed the jars would be emptied into linen sacks already placed in troughs ready to be squeezed to separate the potential wine from the pulp. In my opinion this is part of the process shown in a wall painting from the Old Kingdom tomb of Nefer at Saqqara. Interpretation is not straightforward but it appears that grape pulp in linen sacks is being twisted between two poles to squeeze out the remaining juice. The linen sacking would effectively work as a filter so that no solids are left in the juice. The potential wine would be poured into wine jars, sometimes known as amphorae, having two handles to allow easier lifting and carrying. The jars were then sealed and left until the wine was mature enough to drink. This takes at least six months or more depending upon quality, variety and other factors. Each was labelled, in many cases detailing where produced, date of harvest, name of producer and owner, and often stamped with a royal seal. Wine jars have been found in royal tombs at Abydos and Saqqara which date back to the Early Dynastic period (2950–2575 BC).

Very little is known about the colour of the wine produced in Pharaonic Egypt except in tomb paintings where it is shown as being dark in colour. In an article written by Dr Maria Rosa Guasch Jané, titled "Ancient Egyptian Wine" in the magazine *Ancient Egypt* of June/July 2006 she discusses her research into wine colour. The main problem she encountered was the minimal amount of dry residue available for analysis. The Egyptian Museum in Cairo has many sealed wine jars from Tutankhamun's tomb, some of which are on display. Permission was obtained from the Egyptian Supreme Council for Antiquities to take a small sample of residue from the bottom of an open jar. After developing new methods of analysis she discovered that the wine sample was red.

Withania somnifera

Winter cherry or Withania Nightshade
Family: Solonaceae

An evergreen perennial or low shrub growing 1 to 2 metres high, upright in habit with ovate leaves and hairy stems. The flowers are fairly inconspicuous in small clusters in the leaf axils, and are produced throughout the year. They are mainly green in colour, sometimes shaded yellow. The flower petals when in bud are enclosed by a calyx formed from the green sepals, later followed by yellow-orange berries within the inflated calyx. The plant thrives in stony soils and is often found growing on waste ground in Africa, Egypt and Asia. The berries were frequently used for decorative purposes by the Egyptians, who incorporated them into garlands and wreaths, some of which have been discovered in tombs. It was common practice to attach the berries by thread to the leaves of date palm cut into thin strips to make garlands and wreaths. The root of the plant is used medicinally and is beneficial for the nervous and reproductive systems of the human body. When combined with milk and honey it is taken for insomnia, debility, nervous exhaustion, impotence, infertility and nerve pains.

Zizyphus spina-christi

Christ-thorn

Family: Rhamnaceae

The Christ-thorn is a native of Egypt, and is still cultivated there today, mainly in gardens for its fruit and value as a herbal medicine. It probably grew in Palestine, now Israel, as it is thought to have been used for Jesus' crown of thorns (John 19:2). The fruit and leaves of the Christ-thorn tree were highly valued in Ancient Egypt, and dried fruits have been excavated from predynastic graves. This shrub, or small bushy tree, has several branching stems and twigs tending to have zigzag growth which is whitish-grey. The stems and twigs bear short stalked oval evergreen leaves which are borne alternately along the stem and at the base of each leaf stalk are a pair of needle sharp spines. In the leaf axils clusters of tiny yellow

flowers develop, and later, round red berries are formed which are about the size of cherries. The fruits are edible and sweet apart from the stone, although Pliny claimed that the Egyptians ate the kernel. The timber of the tree was used for carpentry in ancient Egypt as the wood is very durable, and in some cases it was used for coffins. When the fruit was available and dried it could be made into a sort of bread. First the stones were removed before being crushed with a wooden pestle and mortar, water was added and it was then kneaded to make a dough and baked in an oven. As a herbal medicine the leaves of the Christ-thorn were used to treat constipation.

6

YOUR OWN EGYPTIAN GARDEN

The typical ancient Egyptian garden usually included a formal pool, rectangular in shape, placed centrally with paving slabs around it. Often the formal garden was surrounded by high walls constructed of mud bricks for protection from sandstorms driven by strong winds, to keep out stray animals, and for privacy. The perimeter within the walls was planted with trees, often date and doum palms and sycamore figs, to provide shade from the hot sun. The pools were supplied with water from the Nile or its tributaries or lifted from irrigation channels nearby. It seems that pools were typically planted with the white or blue lotus (*Nymphaea lotus* and *Nymphaea caerulea*) and papyrus, and were stocked with fish.

In order to produce an ancient Egyptian garden in the UK it is important to consider the possible problems that are to be overcome in order for it to succeed. The climate of the British Isles is temperate and fairly cool compared with the sub-tropical conditions experienced in Egypt. The plants and trees that thrive in Egypt are more able to withstand dry conditions and for the majority of the year it is so much warmer than the UK. In this country damp and cold winters make it impractical to consider planting many of the native trees and plants of

Egypt. Although winters in the British Isles have become much milder, there is still the possibility of an occasional short cold frosty spell that could severely damage and kill off the more tender plants imported from warmer climates. Today there is speculation as to whether global warming is the reason why winters are milder, but whatever the reason, garden owners can now consider planting sub-tropical species, although it is still a high risk strategy which could result in some expensive losses. It is almost certain that the progress of the warmer winters will be uneven and the occasional hard winter might be experienced. So although it may not be possible to cultivate a garden identical to an ancient Egyptian garden, it is possible to create an ancient Egyptian *themed* garden by choosing plants and trees that can be considered suitable substitutes to give the desired effect.

The site for the garden should be level. If the garden taken as a whole is on a slope then some levelling and terracing will need to be carried out. If possible, avoid hollows and low lying sites which are known frost pockets, and a southerly aspect is preferable. Another consideration is the altitude of the site — for every 250 feet above sea level the temperature drops one degree Fahrenheit. The higher the altitude, the shorter the growing season — just one degree drop in temperature will reduce the season by several days. The garden shown in the plan (see page 172) is orientated to obtain as much sun as possible throughout the day.

Ancient Egyptian gardens were protected by high mud brick walls but to build such a structure is very expensive, and there is no reason why a Yew hedge cannot be used instead. It is true that walled gardens provide a more sheltered environment and during warm sunny days the soil and bricks absorb the heat radiated by the sun, gradually releasing the retained warmth later in the evenings to create a warmer mini-climate. However, during cold frosty days the sheltered garden becomes a frost pocket retaining the cold air for much longer than if there was no shelter. Another problem with solid walls is that they are more likely to be a disadvantage in strong winds, causing plants next to the wall to be flattened due to destructive down draughts. A hedge

allows the wind to flow through, slowing it down and eliminating turbulence. Also, assuming that a garden surrounded by a hedge is not at the bottom of a slope, cold air in the winter will flow through it allowing the colder air to find the lowest level. Frosts in late spring can damage young growth of less hardy plants, shrubs or trees.

The garden may well take three to four years before it looks mature enough. Often it is better to be patient; younger smaller trees and shrubs are easier to establish with less failures. Until a good healthy root system develops, large plants with a lot of foliage have difficulty obtaining enough water to cope with loss through evaporation. I suggest Yew (*Taxus baccata*) to produce a good dense hedge which is evergreen, very hardy and reliable. *Chamaecyparis lawsoniana* species (Lawsons cypress) and *Cupressocyparis leylandii* (Leyland cypress) are faster growing than the Yew and can be trimmed to make a hedge. The problem with Leyland cypress hedges is that they are prone to attack by aphids which can cause the foliage to die, sometimes killing the whole tree. If only a few parts are affected the dead growth can be pruned away but new growth is not readily produced from old wood, leaving unsightly gaps. This is not the case with Yew — it will produce new shoots readily if pruned hard, it is very resistant to pests and diseases and makes a dense hardy hedge. The other advantage is that Yew will grow in well-drained chalky soils (alkaline) that soon dry out. It will tolerate highly acidic soils and most soils in between providing they are well drained. The trees and plants required for the garden prefer well drained soils and I advise avoidance of heavy clay soils which are slow draining. Clay soils are slow to warm up in spring, which reduces the growing season.

The proposed size of garden is 9 metres by 7.2 metres (30 x 24 ft).

In the centre of the garden I suggest the installation of a rectangular pool 360 x 180 cm (12 x 6 ft) x 60 cm deep surrounded by paving 1.2 metres (4 ft) wide. The paving can be either natural stone or a good imitation, preferably honey coloured or darker beige rather than light grey limestone colours. For the pool the ideal solution is to buy a good

THE EGYPTIAN GARDEN

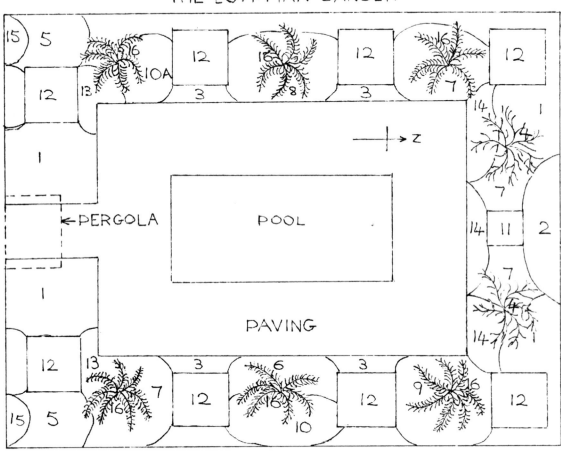

Key to plants used in the plan

Quantities of plants required in brackets after plant name.

1   *Acanthus mollis* (4)

2   *Alcea rosea* Chater's Double or improved modern variety (7)

3   *Chamaemelum nobile* (8)

4   *Ficus carica* (2)

5   *Lilium candidum* (15 bulbs)

6   *Linum usitatissimum* (8)

7   *Lupinus* "Russel Hybrids" — mixed colours (15)

8   *Nigella damascena* (20)

9   *Papaver rhoeas* "Shirley Single Mixed" (20)

10   *Papaver orientale* — Salmon (3)

10A   *Papaver orientale* — Red (2)

11   *Taxus baccata* "Fastigiata" (1)

12   *Taxus baccata* for pyramids (8)

13   *Thymus vulgaris* (4)

14   *Thymus serpyllum* — mixed varieties (12)

15   *Vitis vinifera* "Brandt" or "Madeleine Sylvaner" (2)

16   *Trachycarpus fortunei, T. wagnerianus* or *T. takil* (6)

173

quality liner that will last. Although butyl is expensive, it has a very long life and if properly installed will not leak. To avoid damage to the lining it is necessary to have an under-lining of a type of felt or 'quilt' which will prevent the butyl from being pierced by stones or any other sharp object. To calculate the dimensions of liner required, measure the maximum width of the pool plus twice its depth, by the maximum length plus twice its depth, allowing an extra 15 cm all round. If this formula is followed, a lining measuring 5.1 x 3.3 metres will be required.

Once the site for the garden has been cleared, cultivated and levelled the next task is to measure and mark it out on the ground. For this you will need a large roll of strong twine, a measuring tape at least 10 metres in length, 4 wooden stakes 150 cm x 3 cm and 10 stakes 60 cm x 3 cm. As shown in the plan the two longer sides of the rectangular shaped garden are aligned north to south. Starting at the south end of the site decide where the south east corner of the garden is going to be and tap a 150 cm stake into the ground with a mallet. For accurate alignment it is necessary to have an assistant, and a prismatic compass will be required. Measure 9 metres of twine and allow some extra for tying to a 150 cm stake which will serve as a sighting post. Also it will serve as the north-east corner of the plot. Make sure that the twine is tied to the stake 30 cm up from the base so that the twine is at ground level when the stake is hammered into the ground. The stake must be 9 metres from the first sighting post when tied and held taught, ensuring it is due north using the compass. From this second peg at the north end, measure off at least 7.2 metres of twine and secure to another 150 cm stake, this time taking a sighting with the compass due west. Go back to the first south-east post, repeat the procedure and knock in the post at the south-west corner, then take a sighting with the post at the north-west corner which should be due north. Tie twine to the south-west corner stake and extend to the north-west stake, ensuring twine is taught. Distribute the ten pegs, 3 evenly along the long sides and 2 along the short sides of the boundary of the garden placed alongside the twine attached to the corner posts. These pegs are suggested in

case the line is broken unintentionally or if the line over this long distance becomes slack; it is important to make sure the boundaries are straight and the boundary line is preserved. Make sure the pegs touch the twine without pressing it out of line. This will be needed when planting the yew trees to form a hedge which will create the boundary of the garden.

Making sure the pool and the paving around it is located in the centre of the garden is easily achieved. Take a ball of twine and attach the end to the south-west corner post. Unroll the ball while walking to the north-east post and pull taught. Tie to the post and cut off the remainder. Repeat from the north-west to the south-east corner posts. Where the lines cross in the centre of the garden, put a post or bamboo cane in the ground to mark the spot. By measuring off from this point the outline of the pool and the surrounding pavement can be marked out on the ground with pegs. If the pegs are tapped into the soil so that they are level with the surface they can be used for levelling. It is important to ensure that the pool is level and a suitable tool for this purpose is a laser level. Considering the technology involved they are inexpensive to buy and are supplied with instructions on how to do levelling successfully.

Having marked the outline of the pool and the outline of the paving, which can be measured from the former with pegs and twine, dig out the pool to a depth of 23 cm, trying not to break down the edge. Line the sides with thin wood planking (shuttering) to a depth of 23 cm and knock pegs into the soil to support the shuttering making sure it is level with the pegs used for levelling. Then continue to dig out the soil a further 37 cm to a total depth of 60 cm, leaving a shelf all round of 30 cm, cutting the sides vertically and finishing with a level and flat base. Where the paving is going to go, remove the soil to a depth of 15 cm and make sure that the ground is firm before installing shuttering which should be to a depth of 15 cm. Ensure that the shuttering is up to the outside of the line marking the perimeter of the paving at 120 cm wide. Add 7.5 cm of hard core and on top of that add a further

mixture of concrete which is composed of dry sand and aggregate with the addition of cement in the proportions of 8 to 1. The aggregate and sand can be bought in bags ready mixed. Before you add the concrete it is necessary to reinforce the rim of the pool with mortar so that when the butyl lining is installed the excess of the lining is lapped over the sides and the paving goes on top so that the excess lining is concealed. To form this rim make up a mixture of sand and cement in the proportion of 4 to 1. Add water gradually to this mixture until virtually wet. Apply mortar to the outside edge of the pool shuttering, possibly to a width of 7.5 to 10 cm. Later when you have added the mixture of dry concrete which is firmed and bedded down, level up with the shuttering to the edge of the path and the pool using a board to tamp it down so that it finishes up level with the top edge of the shuttering. Finish off the rim making sure that the mortar is up to the same level and cover the area to be paved with a temporary waterproof cover which should remain until the mortar is set hard. This could take up to 24 hours. Also the temporary waterproof cover is installed to prevent the dry concrete mix for the paving becoming wet before it is laid. To gain access to the pool, put planking down. Once the mortar is set hard remove the shuttering from the pool edge. At this stage the butyl lining can be installed and after this the paving can be laid. The dry mixture of concrete will gather moisture from the soil and atmosphere and will eventually become hard creating a firm foundation. Once the foundation has become hard remove the shuttering. If you remove the shuttering before the concrete is set the edge will collapse.

Having removed the shuttering the protective lining material can be placed in the pond to cover all the surfaces, to prevent damage to the butyl lining placed on top. Take care to avoid breaking down the cement edge when manoeuvring the lining into position, which may require someone to stand on it at some point in the pool. In this case wear soft soled shoes or take them off to avoid piercing the lining. Assuming the lining has been measured correctly there should be an overlap of approximately 15 cm which can be lapped over the cement

edge and the dry cement mix. The paving can be laid onto the black butyl lining which is hardly noticeable when the paving is placed up to the edge of the pool, particularly when the marginal plants are installed. Lay the rest of the paving around the pool.

As shown in the plan, lay 1 metre wide paving as a path to the entrance or exit at the south end of the garden.

At the south end of the garden it is proposed to construct two wooden trellises and a pergola as shown in the diagram and garden plan. The diagram shows a pergola in the centre measuring 120 cm wide with a 300 cm trellis on either side of it. It is proposed that the trellis and pergola should be 210 cm high to support two grape vines.

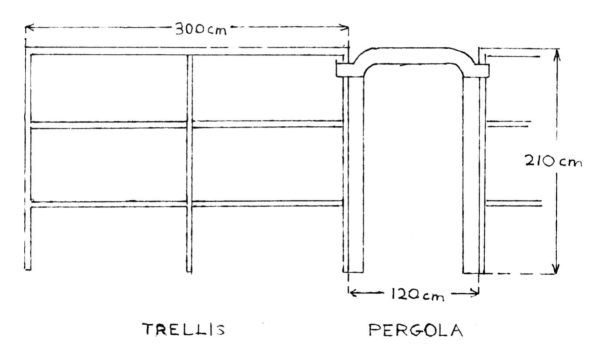

TRELLIS   PERGOLA

Pergolas bearing a resemblance to the design shown in the diagram can be obtained in kit form from garden centres or do-it-yourself stores. Make sure that the timber is pressure treated with preservative so that it will withstand the vagaries of our weather for many years without rotting. However, you might prefer to make your own in which case buy pressure treated timber. In this case purchase fencing posts 7.5 x 7.5 cm and long enough to leave 210 cm out of the ground to be used as the uprights. In order to withstand strong winds dig holes for the posts to a depth of 45 cm insert into the hole and surround the posts with concrete up to and slightly above ground level. Make sure that the concrete slopes from the post to allow any rainwater to run off and away from the post. Before allowing the concrete to set, use a spirit level to check that the posts are vertical both ways. Use posts of the same dimension to provide the upright supports for the trellis and reinforce the bases of the posts in the same way with concrete, but make sure that the posts are erected on the inside of the boundary line.

The pergola is 120 cm x 90 cm with an upright support post at each corner, as shown in the plan. If you have purchased a pergola in kit form the uprights will probably have slots cut into the top of them to hold side rails. Two side rails will be supplied which are placed in the slots, these would probably measure 4 x 7.5 x 90 cm and are held securely in place by bolts or screws. The side rails are necessary to support the three cross beams which will have slots cut into them so that they are securely held by the side rails. Someone sufficiently competent with a saw and a chisel could make the slots themselves for the posts and rails. As a decorative feature the crossbeams overlap the side rails by 15 to 17.5 cm and are shaped as in the diagram. The fence posts for the trellis could have slots cut into the top like the pergola so that a top rail can be fitted 4 x 7.5 x 300 cm. The two lower side rails could also be the same dimensions as the top rails and held securely by cutting slots in the posts and screwing or bolting the side rails to them. To encourage the grape vines to climb over the trellis, support wires will need to be attached to it. When the trellis and pergola has been erected the wood can be stained if this is considered necessary to obtain a more natural colour.

Water Plants

Plants for the pool can be obtained from a water garden specialist which will also supply equipment and fish for the pool if desired. The Egyptian garden pool would have contained the white or blue lotus which are sub tropical water lilies and not suitable for our northern climate, but hardy varieties are available which make a good substitute. It is unfortunate that the Papyrus, which featured heavily in Egyptian gardens, is not hardy enough for the British climate as there is nothing else like it. There are other plants that grow in the margins of river banks in Egypt but they are mainly too tall and too vigorous, however the Reedmace is a more suitable size. To maintain a healthy environment in a pond which has no fresh water flowing into it, oxygenating plants must be provided which prevent the pool becoming stagnant. They are also important if you are planning to stock the pool with fish and help to keep the water clear. The best time to purchase the plants is in spring.

Suitable plants:

Nymphaea marliaca 'Albida' (Water lily) — White, semi-double; flowers 15 to 20 cm across. 5 plants required,
Or
Nymphaea 'Virginalis' (Water lily) — White star shaped flowers; semi-double; free flowering; flowers 10 to 15 cm across. 5 plants required.

Lagarosiphon Major (syn. 'Elodea crispa') — Oxygenating plant. Easy to grow with reflexed leaves (curled back). 24 plants required.

Myriophyllum (commonly called Milfoil) — Oxygenating plant. Has very fine cut leaves giving them a feathery appearance; the stems are very slender. 24 plants required.

179

Marginal plants

Typha domingensis (syn. *Typha australis*) – commonly called Reed-mace or Cat-tail and often mistakenly identified as a bulrush. In the summer it produces a mass of minute flowers formed into brown cylinders, each stem having a male and a female; the male one is uppermost separated by 1–2 cm from the female. The foliage consists of long, mostly erect, leaves about 1 cm wide, up to 1–1.2 metres tall. 3 plants required.

Planting

Water plants should be planted in garden soil that does not contain fertiliser, or in special soil available in bags from water garden suppliers. Suitable containers can also be purchased from them; preformed plastic baskets are ideal for the purpose, but make sure there are no sharp edges that would damage the lining of the pool. The larger baskets are needed for water lilies and when planting, the tubers or roots need only a thin covering of soil allowing the growing points to be exposed.

Lilies benefit from dividing every two to three years, which involves lifting them from the pool, cutting away the old woody tubers and retaining the young growths, cutting off roots to within 15 cm of terminal buds and replanting. Large baskets will be required no more than 23 cm deep for the Reed-mace which tends to be vigorous, forming large clumps of growth. The roots of the plant will need dividing after two years and replanting.

The oxygenating plants are normally bought in small bunches which have weights attached to them, and are usually dropped in the pool where they sink to the bottom. Traditionally it was quite normal to put a 2 to 4 cm layer of soil on the bottom of the pond which the plants could root into. This can be done, but care must be taken to remove any stones or sharp objects that may be contained in it. However, it is much easier later, when it comes to cleaning and replanting the pool, if all the plants are planted in containers. It is a good idea to plant the oxygenating plants in 13 cm clay pots (remove any rough edges) containing soil, putting two bunches in each one. Distribute the pots around the base of the pond, mainly around the sides leaving some open spaces so that fish can be seen. Water the oxygenating plants before filling the pool with water otherwise they may fall over if the soil is dry or only moist.

It is easier to place the plants in the pool, which will involve standing in the pool, before filling with water. It is advisable to wear wellington boots or soft soled shoes while standing on the lining, making sure there is nothing sharp in the treads. Having placed the plants, the pool can be filled with water, preferably slowly so that no soil is washed out of the containers. When filled the water will be cloudy for a few days until the soil settles and the water clears.

Plants Used in the Border Planting Scheme

Chusan Palm (*Trachycarpus fortunei*). Otherwise known as the Windmill Palm, the Chusan Palm has deeply divided fan shaped leaves up to 75 cm long and 90 cm or more wide on long spiny stems at least 90 cm long. The height of the tree varies depending on the climate; in most parts of mainland UK it is capable of exceeding 3.6 metres. In the south west and western coastal areas which benefit from the Gulf Stream it is possible for a mature specimen to reach 12 metres with a spread of 3.6 metres but this could take many decades. It is advisable to provide a sheltered position for this palm as the leaves are liable to be damaged by strong winds. The leaves are clustered at the top of a stout cylindrical trunk which is covered in the fibrous remains of the old leaf bases. The tree is quite hardy and able to thrive in winter temperatures down to -12 °C.

Alternatives to the Chusan Palm include *Trachycarpus takil*, which is very similar in growth and appearance to *T. fortunei* but is hardier, withstanding winter temperatures of -14 °C, or *T. wagnerianus*, which is also very similar to *T. fortunei* except it is a dwarf form but is resistant to strong winds and at least as hardy.

The Canary Palm (*Phoenix canariensis*) is almost identical to the date palm, having long pinnate leaves, and makes a large tree with a spread of 6 to 10 metres. It is slow growing in this country but eventually too big for the average large garden, although, perhaps, ideal for a park or large estate.

The Australian Cabbage Palm (*Cordyline australis*) has long narrow strap shaped leaves, and although they are not divided, it has a similar appearance to a palm tree particularly when the stem base is bare of leaves. Not as hardy as the palms mentioned above, but can be protected from the coldest part of the winter by lifting the leaves and tying in an upright position, wrapping with straw and covering with an outer layer of hessian. This small tree and the palms tend to drop the lowest leaves as they grow, and gradually the length of bare stem increases with the majority of the green leaves near the top of the tree.

Common English Yew (*Taxus baccata*). A native evergreen conifer that makes a bushy wide-spreading tree generally small to medium in size, although some reach a very old age growing up to 18 metres high. The leaves are narrow, up to 3 cm long, very dark green, almost black, on the upper surface and lighter green underneath. Occasionally the yew bears soft red berries about 6–7 mm in size. Will grow in shade or full sun and makes an ideal hedge when trimmed. *T. baccata* "Fastigiata", the Irish Yew, has dense narrow to columnar growth when young.

An alternative for the pyramids is the Box (*Buxus sempervirens*), an evergreen shrub or small evergreen tree with dark green leaves almost circular in shape and densely arranged on short stems.

Common Fig (*Ficus carica* "Brown Turkey"). Pear shaped fruit, brownish-green when ripe, this variety is self-fertile and is capable of bearing fruit in the UK. Will thrive in winter in temperatures down to -12 °C (10 °F).

Grape (*Vitis vinifera*). "Madeleine Sylvaner" produces white grapes good enough for eating when grown in mild areas, but in cooler areas of Britain it is more suitable for wine. "Brandt" produces small black grapes capable of making a good rosé wine. In the autumn the green leaves develop attractive shades of russet and purple before falling.

Acanthus mollis produces clusters of leaves up to 1 metre long and 20 cm wide, deeply lobed, frequently featured in designs of the past. Thought to have inspired Roman architects to feature the leaves of this plant on Corinthian column capitals. Produces tubular flowers that can be lilac, rose or white, usually with purplish spiny bracts attached to tall spikes of flowers on sturdy stems growing up to 180 to 240 cm. Flowers in early summer.

Alcea rosea (Common Hollyhock). "Chater's Hybrids" is a double flowered variety developed in the nineteenth century from the single flowered species introduced to Britain from the Middle East. A variety of colours are available including pink shades, lemon, yellow, white and maroon. A summer flowering perennial which is sometimes short lived growing up to 2.4 metres with a spread of 45–60 cm.

Roman Chamomile (*Chamaemelum nobile*). Roman chamomile is sometimes known by the name of *Anthemis nobilis*. This plant was known in ancient Egypt and associated with Egyptian gods. Tends to form mats of growth, with leaves attached alternately, downy and finely divided up to 5 cm long. It has the occasional solitary flower on a stem up to 20 cm with yellow discs and white ray florets during the summer. Grows up to 15 cm high with a spread of 45 cm, and is often planted as a lawn because of the strong apple scent when trodden on.

Madonna Lily (*Lilium candidum*). A perennial bulb producing up to 20 pure white flowers, shaded yellow inside the base and having a fragrant scent. Height 1 to 1.5 metres, spread 30 to 45 cm.

Flax (*Linum usitatissimum*). A summer flowering annual with sky blue flowers, erect growth, leaves grey-green up to 2.5 cm long. Height is at least 80 cm with a spread of 30–60 cm. Sow direct into the border having prepared the soil in March or April, and later thin out the seedlings.

Lupin (*Lupinus* species). In some Mediterranean countries and Egypt lupin beans are eaten, soaked in salty water. The Romans cultivated lupins, introducing them to all parts of the Roman Empire. Mediterranean species are also used to feed livestock and poultry. The Mediterranean species are probably not ideal for our climate. I suggest the ideal lupins for the British climate are the Russell hybrids, which grow to a height of 75–90 cm with a spread of 45 to 60 cm, flowering June to July. They tend to be short lived, so replace every 3 to 4 years. Like most lupins the leaves are palmate divided into 8–20 leaflets and a mass of flowers are produced in tall spikes with pea flower shape, each flower 1–2 cm long.

Love-in-a-mist (*Nigella damascena*). Suggested as a substitute for *Nigella sativa*. *Nigella damascena* is very similar but more suitable for providing a good display of flowers which come in blue shades, though dark blue is the original colour. Has finely divided pinnate leaves with a feathery appearance. At a distance away, the flowers appear to be wreathed in a slight mist. An annual plant, it is fairly erect up to 45 cm high with a spread of 25 cm. Seeds are sown direct into prepared soil during March or early April and thinned out later when the seedlings are large enough to handle.

Papaver rhoeas. "Shirley Single Mixed" is a cultivated strain of the Flanders poppy or corn poppy developed during the nineteenth century. An annual plant up to 60 cm high with a spread of 30 cm available from seed usually providing flowers in shades of crimson, rose, salmon, pink and white during the summer. Seeds are sown direct into prepared soil during March or early April and thinned out later when seedlings are large enough to handle.

Oriental Poppy (*Papaver orientale*). A herbaceous perennial very similar to the annual opium poppy with regard to the flowers, although they are slightly larger and some varieties are double-flowered and having a wider range of colours; available in pink, red, crimson, salmon, lilac, cream and white. The flowers are produced during the summer, later developing large seed capsules, like a pepper pot. Has large wavy leaves, fairly rough to feel due to leaf hairs, pinnate up to 40 cm in length. Makes a large plant up to 90 cm high with a spread of 60–90 cm flowering May and June.

Common Thyme (*Thymus vulgaris*). A small variable shrub with wiry stems and growth tending to be fairly open. Has tiny grey-green leaves with pale flowers, sometimes white, attractive to bees when flowering in summer. Height 30–45 cm with a spread of 60 cm. It is used for flavouring in cooking.

Creeping Thyme (*Thymus serpyllum*). This species is very low growing and will withstand being walked on, although not recommended too often. Like many of the cultivated varieties it forms mats of growth, and can grow to a height of 7 cm, with a spread of 45–90 cm. Some of the varieties have variegated leaves which can be green and gold, greenish-yellow, or tinted bronze which could be useful in mixed plantings of thymes. The flowers can be white and also come in shades of pink, rose, mauve and purple. The flowers usually last for one month in the summer season.

Explanation of Planting Scheme

As shown in the plan the Chusan palm has been chosen as it bears some resemblance to the Date or Doum palm which featured in ancient Egyptian gardens. There are a small number of nurseries that produce hardy palms in the UK. Apart from the yews used for hedging, a further eight, possibly 120 cm tall, are planted where indicated in the plan to be trained into a pyramidal shape. The alternative for this purpose is box (*Buxus sempervirens*) which like the yew is evergreen and can be trimmed to the desired shape. The plants for this purpose are best selected individually to have a bushy habit which would lend themselves to this purpose. In addition, one yew (*Taxus baccata* "Fastigiata") is to be planted where indicated to be trimmed into a narrowly pyramidal shape to represent 'Cleopatra's Needle' which many readers will know is on the Embankment of the Thames in London.

The figs are planted in the open which is quite safe in milder more favoured areas as far north as the Midlands and western coastal regions warmed by the Gulf Stream. Further north it would be wise to grown them fan-trained against a wall facing south or west. The fig prefers well drained soil, and tends to be a vigorous grower that needs to have a restricted root system, otherwise it may not bear fruit. This is best achieved by building a brick barrier about 60 x 60 cm and 60 cm deep and planting with unfertilised garden soil mixed with plenty of grit to improve drainage.

For the yew hedge, 42 trees will be needed 1–1.2 metres in height which can be purchased as bare rooted plants in late autumn, although there is always a risk of some losses particularly if the roots become dried out in transit from a nursery. These days most nurseries or garden centres sell them in plastic pots and they can be planted where required without root disturbance. To form a good hedge, plant 60 cm apart, and once established cut back the main shoot by 2 cm.

To make the garden more authentic it may be possible to obtain, or

commission a specialist to make, a Sphinx replica to place on the paving in front of the *Taxus baccata* "Fastigiata".

I recommend purchasing the *RHS Plant Finder*, which will help if there is a problem finding any of the plants.

BIBLIOGRAPHY

ANDREWS, Carol, *Ancient Egyptian Jewellery*, British Museum Press, 1990

BARWANI, Ali, 'Figs Are What They Used To Be' in *The Lady*, 6–12 February 2007, London

BATANOUNY, K H (ed.), *Encyclopaedia of Wild Medicinal Plants in Egypt*, Vol. 1, Project of Conservations and Sustainable Use of Medicinal Plants in Arid and Semi-Arid Ecosystems Egypt, Cairo, 2005

BELLINGER, Kay, *Nothing New Under the Sun*, Amarna Publishing, Sheffield, 2005

BIRCHER, Warda H., *Gardens of the Hesperides: A book on old and new plants for Egypt and similar climes*, Anglo Egyptian Bookshop, Cairo, 1960

BOND, James, *Monastic Landscapes*, Tempus Publishing Limited, Stroud, 2004

BRICKELL, Christopher (ed.), *The Royal Horticultural Society Encyclopaedia of Gardening*, Dorling Kindersley Publishers Limited, London, 1996

BOWN, Deni, *RHS Encyclopaedia of Herbs and Their Uses*, Dorling Kindersley Limited, London, 1995

BREASTED, J. H., *Historic Egypt*, 1905

BROOKES, John, *Gardens of Paradise: History and Design of the Great Islamic Gardens*, Weidenfeld & Nicholson, London, 1987

CAMPBELL, Colin, *The Gardener's Tomb (Sen-nofer's) at Thebes*, J MacLehose & Sons, Glasgow, 1908

DAWSON, Warren K., 'Studies in The Egyptian Medical Texts – II', in *The Journal of Egyptian Archaeology*, Volume XVIII, p.150-4

DELL, Linda Louisa, 'Ancient Aroma' in *The Lady*, 25–31 July 2006, London

FARRAR, Linda, *Ancient Roman Gardens*, Sutton Publishing Ltd., Stroud, 1998

HAMILTON, Geoff, *'Gardeners World' Practical Gardening Course*, BBC Books, London, 1993

HANTELMANN, Christa von, (ed.), *Gardens of Delight: The Great Islamic Gardens*, New Line Books, 2005

HEPPER, F. Nigel, *Pharaoh's Flowers: Botanical Treasures of Tutankhamen*, Stationery Office Books, London, 1990

HEPPER, F. Nigel, *Baker Encyclopaedia of Bible Plants: Flowers and Trees, Fruits and Vegetables, Ecology*, Baker Pub Group, 1993

HEPPER, F. Nigel, 'An Ancient Expedition to Transplant Living Trees: Exotic Gardening by An Egyptian Queen', reprinted from *The Journal of The Royal Horticultural Society*, Volume XCII Part 10, October 1967

HILLIER, Harold G., *Hillier's Manual of Trees and Shrubs*, David & Charles, Newton Abbot, 5th edition, 1981

HOBHOUSE, Penelope, *Plants in Garden History*, Pavilion Books Ltd., London, 1992

JANÉ, Dr Maria Rosa Guasch, 'Ancient Egyptian Wine' in *Ancient Egypt*, (ed. Bob Partridge), Empire Publications, Manchester, June/July 2006, No 36

JENNINGS, Anne, *Medieval Gardens*, English Heritage, London, 2004

JOHNSON, Hugh, *The Principles of Gardening: The Science, Practice and History of the Gardener's Art*, Mitchell Beazley Publishers Limited, London, 1979

LEHRMAN, Jonas, Earthly Paradise: Courtyard and Garden in Islam, Thames & Hudson, 1980

LICHTHEIM, Miriam, *Ancient Egyptian Literature: A Book of Readings: New Kingdom vol. 2*, University of California Press Ltd, 1973

MAIURI, Amedeo, *Pompeii*, Instituto Geografico De Agostini, Novara, Italy, 1957

MANNICHE, Lise, *An Ancient Egyptian Herbal*, British Museum Press, London, 1999

MOYNIHAN, Elizabeth B., *Paradise As a Garden: In Persia and Mughal India*, George Braziller, New York, 1980

MURRAY, Dr Margaret A., *The Splendour That Was Egypt*, Sidgwick and Jackson, London, 1931

NIBBI, Alessandra, "A Fresh Look at the Egyptian Environment of the Pharaonic Period", *Palestine Exploration Quarterly*, 1981

NICHOLSON, Paul T., *Egyptian Faience and Glass*, Shire Publications, 1993

NUNN, John F., *Ancient Egyptian Medicine*, British Museum Press, 1997

OTTO DE GARCIA, Karen, *The Alhambra and the Generalife*, Ricardo Villa-Real, 1982

SHAW, Ian, and NICHOLSON , Paul T., *British Museum Dictionary of Ancient Egypt*, British Museum Press, London, 1995

PEET, Eric T., *The City of Akhenaten*, Egypt Exploration Society, 1923

PERRY, Frances, *Collins Guide to Border Plants: Hardy Herbaceous Plants*, Collins, London, 1966

PERRY, Frances, *Water Gardens*, Penguin Books Ltd, 1962

SANDERS, Thomas William, MACSELF, A. J., *Sanders Encyclopaedia of Gardening*, W. H. & L. Collingridge Limited, London, 1931

SILVERMAN, David P, *50 Wonders of Tutankhamun*, Crown Publishers Inc., New York, 1978

SMITH, W. Stevenson, *The Art and Architecture of Ancient Egypt*, Penguin Books, 1958

STRUDWICK, Nigel, *Masterpieces of Ancient Egypt*, British Museum Press, London, 2006

TOOGOOD, Alan R., *Collins Garden Trees Handbook: A Complete Guide to Choosing, Planting, and Caring for Garden Trees*, Collins, London, 1990

TYLDESLEY, Joyce A., *The Private Lives of The Pharaohs*, Channel 4 Books, London, 2000

TYLER-WHITTLE, Michael, *The Plant Hunters*, William Heinemann Ltd., London, 1970

WALKER, Winifred, *All the Plants of the Bible*, Doubleday & Company Inc., New York, 1979

WATT, Martin, & Wanda Sellar, *Frankincense and Myrrh: Through the Ages and a Complete Guide to Their Use in Herbalism and Aromatherapy Today*, C W Daniel, 1996

WILSON, Hilary, 'Papyrus: Myth and Symbolism', in *Ancient Egypt*, (ed. Bob Partridge), Empire Publications, Manchester, December 2004/January 2005, No. 27

WITHERS, Percy, *Egypt of Yesterday and Today*, Grant Richards, London, 1909

List of Illustrations

All illustrations are by the author, except for those listed below:

p.8 Early Egyptians using a system of weights and poles called shadufs to get water from the Nile by Peter Jackson (1922-2003). (© Look and Learn / The Bridgeman Art Library).

p.14 An ancient Egyptian garden (engraving) (b/w photo) by Egyptian School. (The Stapleton Collection / The Bridgeman Art Library).

p.15 Model of villa and garden of Meketre. (Robert Partridge: The Ancient Egyptian Picture Library).

p.17 Garden of a private estate with an ornamental pool, part of the wall painting from the Tomb of Nebamun, Thebes, New Kingdom, c.1350 BC (painted plaster) by Egyptian 18th Dynasty (c.1567–1320 BC). (British Museum, London, UK / The Bridgeman Art Library).

p.19 Garden of a High Ranking Egyptian Dignitary, from 'I Monumenti dell'Egitto e della Nubia' by Ippolito Rossellini (1800–43), published 1834 (colour litho) by Italian School (19th century). (The Stapleton Collection / The Bridgeman Art Library).

p.22 Overview of Mentuhotep's Temple. (Robert Partridge: The Ancient Egyptian Picture Library).

p.23 Loading myrrh trees on a ship in Punt, after a relief in Queen Hatshepsut's temple at Deir el-Bahri. (Robert Partridge: The Ancient Egyptian Picture Library).

pp.24–25 Painted pavement from The Great Palace complex at Amarna (reproduced from Eric T. Peet, *The City of Akhenaten*, Egypt Exploration Society, 1923).

p.26 Painted grapes from the ceiling of The Great Palace complex at Amarna (reproduced from Eric T. Peet, *The City of Akhenaten*, Egypt Exploration Society, 1923).

p.27 Painted column from the Maru-Aten (reproduced from Eric T. Peet, *The City of Akhenaten*, Egypt Exploration Society, 1923).

p.29 The Great Palace — isometric drawing of the North Harem restored (reproduced from Eric T. Peet, *The City of Akhenaten*, Egypt Exploration Society, 1923).

p.33 The Hanging Gardens of Babylon, from a series of the 'Seven Wonders of the World' published in 'Munchener Bilderbogen', 1886 (colour litho) by Knab, Ferdinand (1834-1902). (Archives Charmet / The Bridgeman Art Library).

p.55 The Patio de la Acequia (Court of the Long Pond). Photograph © Andrew Dunn, 11 May 2006. Website: www.andrewdunnphoto.com.

p.63 Trumpet and wooden stopper, from the Tomb of Tutankhamun (c.1370–1352 BC) New Kingdom (bronze or copper with gold overlay) by Egyptian 18th Dynasty (c.1567–1320 BC). (Egyptian National Museum, Cairo, Egypt / Photo © Boltin Picture Library / The Bridgeman Art Library).

p.65 End panel of Wooden Casket from King Tutankhamun's Tomb. (Robert Partridge: The Ancient Egyptian Picture Library).

p.66 Ointment spoon (painted ivory) (Egyptian Brooklyn Museum of Art, New York, USA / The Bridgeman Art Library).

p.67 Gold earrings found in Sety II's tomb. (Robert Partridge: The Ancient Egyptian Picture Library).

p.68 Faience Collar from 18th Dynasty. (Robert Partridge: The Ancient Egyptian Picture Library).

p.103 Picture of Papyrus from Ancient Egypt magazine. (Robert Partridge: The Ancient Egyptian Picture Library).

p.107 Engaged Papyrus columns in the buildings of Djoser at Saqqara. (Robert Partridge: The Ancient Egyptian Picture Library).

All line drawings of plants in Chapter 5 are primarily from woodcuts of the 16th and 19th centuries, and copper engravings or lithographs from the 19th century.

Printed in the United Kingdom
by Lightning Source UK Ltd.
134261UK00002B/24/P